TEACHER RECOMMENDED

5th GRADE COMMON CORE MATH
DAILY PRACTICE WORKBOOK

PART I: MULTIPLE CHOICE

ARGOPREP.COM

FREE ONLINE SYSTEM WITH VIDEO EXPLANATIONS

ArgoPrep is one of the leading providers of supplemental educational products and services. We offer affordable and effective test prep solutions to educators, parents and students. Learning should be fun and easy! For that reason, most of our workbooks come with detailed video answer explanations taught by one of our fabulous instructors.

Our goal is to make your life easier, so let us know how we can help you by e-mailing us at: info@argoprep.com.

ALL RIGHTS RESERVED
Copyright © 2022 by Argo Brothers, Inc.

ISBN: 978-1951048877
Published by Argo Brothers, Inc.

All rights reserved, no part of this book may be reproduced or distributed in any form or by any means without the written permission of Argo Brothers, Inc.
All the materials within are the exclusive property of Argo Brothers, Inc.

ArgoPrep has won **over 10+ educational awards** for their workbooks and online learning platform. Here are a few highlighted awards!

TABLE OF CONTENTS

Week 1 - *Place value* 10

Week 2 - *Expanded form vs standard form* 17

Week 3 - *Rounding numbers* 23

Week 4 - *Decimals* 29

Week 5 - *Converting phrases into algebraic expressions* 35

Week 6 - *Comparing number patterns* 41

Week 7 - *Fractions* 47

Week 8 - *Fraction word problems* 53

Week 9 - *Division problems* 58

Week 10 - *Multiplying fractions by whole numbers* 65

Week 11 - *Understanding products based on factors* 71

Week 12 - *Real world word problems* 77

Week 13 - *Working with unit fractions* 83

Week 14 - *Converting units* 89

Week 15 - *Understanding dot plots* 95

Week 16 - *Volume of three-dimensional shapes* 101

Week 17 - *Volume (continued)* 107

Week 18 - *Volume word problems* 113

Week 19 - *Graphing points on a coordinate plane* 119

Week 20 - *Understanding characteristics of shapes* 125

End of Year Assessment 132

Answer Key 143

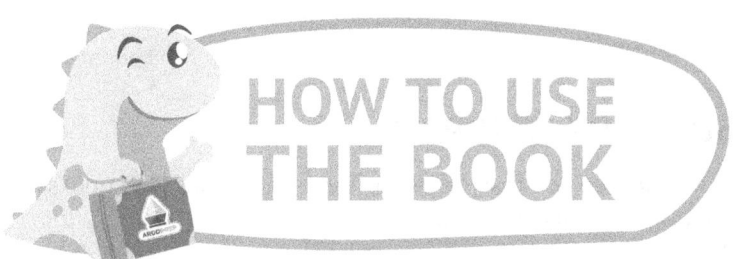

HOW TO USE THE BOOK

This workbook is designed to give lots of practice with the math Common Core State Standards (CCSS). By practicing and mastering this entire workbook, your child will become very familiar and comfortable with the state math exam. If you are a teacher using this workbook for your students, you will notice each question is labeled with the specific standard so you can easily assign your students problems in the workbook. This workbook takes the CCSS and divides them up among 20 weeks. By working on these problems on a daily basis, students will be able to (1) find any deficiencies in their understanding and/or practice of math and (2) have small successes each day that will build proficiency and confidence in their abilities.

We strongly recommend watching the videos as they will reinforce the fundamental concepts. Please note, scrap paper may be necessary while using this workbook so that the student has sufficient space to show their work.

For a detailed overview of the Common Core State Standards for 5th grade, please visit: www.corestandards.org/Math/Content/5/introduction/

HOW TO WATCH VIDEO EXPLANATIONS
IT IS ABSOLUTELY FREE

Download our app:
ArgoPrep Video Explanations
to access videos on any mobile device or tablet.

or

Step 1 - Visit our website at: www.argoprep.com/k8
Step 2 - Click on the "Video Explanations" button located on the top right corner.
Step 3 - Choose the workbook you have and enjoy video explanations.

You can scan this QR code to access video explanations as well.

OTHER BOOKS BY ARGOPREP

Here are some other test prep workbooks by ArgoPrep you may be interested in. All of our workbooks come equipped with detailed video explanations to make your learning experience a breeze! Visit us at **www.argoprep.com**

COMMON CORE MATH SERIES

COMMON CORE ELA SERIES

INTRODUCING MATH!

Introducing Math! by ArgoPrep is an award-winning series created by certified teachers to provide students with high-quality practice problems. Our workbooks include topic overviews with instruction, practice questions, answer explanations along with digital access to video explanations. Practice in confidence - with ArgoPrep!

SCIENCE SERIES

Science Daily Practice Workbook by ArgoPrep is an award-winning series created by certified science teachers to help build mastery of foundational science skills. Our workbooks explore science topics in depth with ArgoPrep's 5 E'S to build science mastery.

KIDS SUMMER ACADEMY SERIES

ArgoPrep's Kids Summer Academy series helps prevent summer learning loss and gets students ready for their new school year by reinforcing core foundations in math, english and science. Our workbooks also introduce new concepts so students can get a head start and be on top of their game for the new school year!

WATER FIRE

MYSTICAL NINJA

GREEN POISON

FIRESTORM WARRIOR

RAPID NINJA

CAPTAIN ARGO

THUNDER WARRIOR

DANCE HERO

ADRASTOS THE SUPER WARRIOR

CAPTAIN BRAVERY

For more practice with 5th Grade Math, be sure to check out our other book, Common Core Math Workbook Grade 5: Free Response

WEEK 1

Congratulations on choosing to work at becoming a better math student! It starts here with Week 1, where you will learn about how digits have different values according to their location in a number.

You can find detailed video explanations of each problem in the book by visiting: ArgoPrep.com

WEEK 1 : DAY 1

1. How many times greater is the value of the digit 7 in 75,608 than the value of the digit 7 in 439,716?

   A. 10 times
   B. 100 times
   C. 1,000 times
   D. $\frac{1}{10}$ times

   5.NBT.1

2. The digit 4 in 104,682 is _____ times the value of the 4 in 45,709.

   A. 10
   B. 100
   C. $\frac{1}{10}$
   D. $\frac{1}{100}$

   5.NBT.1

3. In which of the following numbers does the 5 have a value that is $\frac{1}{10}$ the value of the 5 in 95,126?

   A. 194,538
   B. 570,412
   C. 236,985
   D. 854,427

   5.NBT.1

4. The number 413.86 is given. In a different number, the 8 represents a value which is one-tenth of the value of the 8 in 413.86. What value is represented by the 8 in the other number?

   A. eight hundredths
   B. eight tenths
   C. eight ones
   D. eight tens

   5.NBT.1

5. The digit 1 in 524,681 is _____ times the value of the 1 in 94,130.

   A. 10
   B. 100
   C. $\frac{1}{10}$
   D. $\frac{1}{100}$

   5.NBT.1

6. How many times greater is the value of the digit 8 in 8,642 than the value of the digit 8 in 47,518?

   A. 10 times
   B. 100 times
   C. 1,000 times
   D. 10,000 times

   5.NBT.1

If the same digit is in the tens and hundreds places, the digit in the tens place is $\frac{1}{10}$ the value of that same digit in the hundreds place.

WEEK 1 : DAY 2

1. In which of the following numbers does the 9 have a value that is $\frac{1}{10}$ the value of the 9 in 9,860,112?

   A. 594,738
   B. 649,412
   C. 247,925
   D. 954,870

   5.NBT.1

2. How many times greater is the value of the digit 1 in 81,302 than the value of the digit 1 in 47,518?

   A. 10 times
   B. 100 times
   C. 1,000 times
   D. 10,000 times

   5.NBT.1

The table below shows the number of visitors to a park on certain days. Use the table to answer questions 3 – 5.

Tuesday	184,263
Wednesday	218,136
Friday	381,642
Sunday	623,481

3. Which day has a 4 that is 100 times the value of the digit 4 in 7,145?

   A. Tuesday
   B. Wednesday
   C. Friday
   D. Sunday

   5.NBT.1

4. Which day has a 3 that is $\frac{1}{10}$ the value of the digit 3 in 130,768?

   A. Tuesday
   B. Wednesday
   C. Friday
   D. Sunday

   5.NBT.1

5. Which day has an 8 that is $\frac{1}{100}$ the value of the digit 8 in 859,705?

   A. Tuesday
   B. Wednesday
   C. Friday
   D. Sunday

   5.NBT.1

TIP of the DAY

Digits that lie to the right of another digit are smaller than that digit (the digit to their left). The 4 in 14 is $\frac{1}{10}$ the size of the 4 in 46.

WEEK 1 : DAY 3

1. The number 254.96 is given. In a different number, the 5 represents a value which is one-tenth of the value of the 5 in 254.96. What value is represented by the 5 in the other number?

   A. five hundredths
   B. five tenths
   C. five ones
   D. five tens

   5.NBT.1

2. The digit 9 in 5,063,791 is ____ times the value of the 9 in 4,729,513.

   A. 10
   B. 100
   C. $\frac{1}{10}$
   D. $\frac{1}{100}$

   5.NBT.1

3. How many times greater is the value of the digit 2 in 82,351 than the value of the digit 2 in 67,208?

   A. 10 times
   B. 100 times
   C. 1,000 times
   D. 10,000 times

   5.NBT.1

4. Which term can be put in the blank to make the statement true?

   50,000 = 50 _____

   A. thousands
   B. ten-thousands
   C. hundred-thousands
   D. millions

   5.NBT.1

5. In which of the following numbers does the 7 have a value that is $\frac{1}{10}$ the value of the 7 in 1,460,273?

   A. 90,735
   B. 17,649
   C. 15,627
   D. 28,376

   5.NBT.1

6. The digit 2 in 5,024,687 is ____ times the value of the 2 in 10,210.

   A. 10
   B. 100
   C. $\frac{1}{10}$
   D. $\frac{1}{100}$

   5.NBT.1

TIP of the DAY

If the same digit is in the hundreds and thousands places, the digit in the thousands place is 10 times the value of that same digit in the hundreds place.

14

WEEK 1 : DAY 4

1. The digit 1 in 521,634 is _____ times the value of the 1 in 195,837.

    A. 10
    B. 100
    C. $\frac{1}{10}$
    D. $\frac{1}{100}$

    5.NBT.1

2. Which term can be put in the blank to make the statement true?

    400,000 = 40 _____

    A. thousands
    B. ten-thousands
    C. hundred-thousands
    D. millions

    5.NBT.1

3. Which number is the product of 37.816 and 100?

    A. 3781.6
    B. 378.16
    C. 37.816
    D. 3.7816

    5.NBT.2

4. Which expression is the same as 14×10^4?

    A. 1,400
    B. 14,000
    C. 140,000
    D. 1,400,000

    5.NBT.2

5. What is the quotient when 2014.86 is divided by 1,000?

    A. 2,014,860
    B. 201,486
    C. 201.486
    D. 2.01486

    5.NBT.2

6. Which expression is equivalent to 10,000?

    A. 10^1
    B. 10^2
    C. 10^3
    D. 10^4

    5.NBT.2

Remember the difference between one ten (1 × 10) and one tenth $\left(1 \times \frac{1}{10}\right)$.

WEEK 1 : DAY 5

ASSESSMENT

1. The digit 3 in 723,654 is _____ times the value of the 3 in 935,701.

   A. 10
   B. 100
   C. $\frac{1}{10}$
   D. $\frac{1}{100}$

   5.NBT.1

2. Which term can be put in the blank to make the statement true?

   9,000,000 = 90 _____

   A. thousands
   B. ten-thousands
   C. hundred-thousands
   D. millions

   5.NBT.1

3. What is 0.0681 × 1,000?

   A. 68.1
   B. 6.81
   C. 681
   D. 6,810

   5.NBT.2

4. Which number is the product of 7.16 and 10,000?

   A. 7.160000
   B. 716.0000
   C. 71,600
   D. 7,160

   5.NBT.2

5. What is the quotient when 5,014.863 is divided by 10^3?

   A. 5014.863
   B. 501.4863
   C. 50.14863
   D. 5.014863

   5.NBT.2

6. In which of the following numbers does the 8 have a value that is $\frac{1}{100}$ the value of the 8 in 389,152?

   A. 974,835
   B. 348,402
   C. 487,925
   D. 854,730

   5.NBT.1

DAY 6
Challenge question

A. What is 14,968 when multiplied by a) 100 and b) 10,000?
B. What is 14,968 when it is divided by a) 100 and b) 10,000?

5.NBT.2

16

In Week 2, you will practice writing numbers in different ways - in expanded form, in words, and in standard form.

You can find detailed video explanations of each problem in the book by visiting: ArgoPrep.com

WEEK 2 : DAY 1

1. Which expression is the same as 68×10^2?
   A. 6,800
   B. 68,000
   C. 680,000
   D. 6,800,000

   5.NBT.2

2. What is 7.563 × 1,000?
   A. 7.563000
   B. 75.36
   C. 753.6
   D. 7,563

   5.NBT.2

3. Which expression is equivalent to 60,000?
   A. 6×10^2
   B. 6×10^3
   C. 6×10^4
   D. 6×10^5

   5.NBT.2

4. Which term can be put in the blank to make the statement true?

   180,000 = 18 _____

   A. thousands
   B. ten-thousands
   C. hundred-thousands
   D. millions

   5.NBT.1

5. What is 320.76 divided by 100?
   A. 3.2076
   B. 32.076
   C. 320.76
   D. 3207.6

   5.NBT.2

6. Which expression is the same as 4.96×10^3?
   A. 4.96000
   B. 49.6
   C. 496
   D. 4,960

   5.NBT.2

TIP of the DAY: When multiplying by a power of 10, don't forget your product should be a larger number.

WEEK 2 : DAY 2

1. Which term can be put in the blank to make the statement true?

   7,600,000 = 76 _____

   A. thousands
   B. ten-thousands
   C. hundred-thousands
   D. millions

   5.NBT.1

2. What is 14,928 divided by 10^2?

   A. 1492.8
   B. 149.28
   C. 14.928
   D. 1.498

   5.NBT.2

3. $(9 \times 100{,}000) + (5 \times 10{,}000) + (6 \times 1{,}000) + (8 \times 100) + (1 \times 10) + \left(2 \times \frac{1}{10}\right) + \left(5 \times \frac{1}{100}\right)$

   Which number below is one-hundredth of the expanded form above?

   A. 9568102.5
   B. 956810.25
   C. 95681.025
   D. 9568.1025

   5.NBT.3

4. Which number is equal to forty-one hundred ten and five thousandths?

   A. 4,110,010.005
   B. 410,010.05
   C. 4,110.005
   D. 4,110.05

   5.NBT.3

5. Which expression shows 524.16 in expanded form?

   A. $(5 \times 100) + (2 \times 10) + (4 \times 1) + \left(1 \times \frac{1}{10}\right) + \left(6 \times \frac{1}{100}\right)$
   B. $(5 \times 100) + (2 \times 10) + (4 \times 1) + \left(1 \times \frac{1}{1}\right) + \left(6 \times \frac{1}{10}\right)$
   C. $(5 \times 1000) + (2 \times 10) + (4 \times 1) + \left(1 \times \frac{1}{10}\right) + \left(6 \times \frac{1}{100}\right)$
   D. $(5 \times 100) + (2 \times 100) + (4 \times 1) + \left(1 \times \frac{1}{100}\right) + \left(6 \times \frac{1}{10}\right)$

   5.NBT.3

6. Which statement below is true?

   A. seventy-five hundredths < three tenths
   B. 12 thousands = 0.012
   C. $5(10) + 4(1) + 8\left(\frac{1}{100}\right) = 54.08$
   D. twelve and ninety-one thousandths > twelve and six tenths

   5.NBT.3

TIP of the DAY

Before working on math, gather all materials you might need such as lots of paper, pencils, as well as a protractor and/or ruler.

WEEK 2 : DAY 3

1. $(1 \times 10{,}000) + (5 \times 1{,}000) + (4 \times 100) + (3 \times 10) + (6 \times 1) + \left(8 \times \dfrac{1}{10}\right) + \left(7 \times \dfrac{1}{100}\right)$

   Which number below is one-tenth of the expanded form above?

   A. 1543.687
   B. 15436.87
   C. 154368.7
   D. 1543687

   5.NBT.1
   5.NBT.3

2. Which expression is equivalent to 300,000?

   A. 3×10^2
   B. 3×10^3
   C. 3×10^4
   D. 3×10^5

   5.NBT.2

3. Look at 51.368. In a different number, the 6 represents a value which is one-tenth of the value of the 6 in 51.368. What value is represented by the 6 in the other number?

   A. six thousandths
   B. six hundredths
   C. six tenths
   D. six ones

   5.NBT.1

4. $(3 \times 10{,}000) + (5 \times 1{,}000) + (9 \times 100) + (7 \times 10) + (6 \times 1) + \left(7 \times \dfrac{1}{10}\right) + \left(8 \times \dfrac{1}{100}\right)$

   Which number below is one-tenth of the expanded form above?

   A. 359.7678
   B. 3597.678
   C. 35976.78
   D. 359767.8

   5.NBT.1
   5.NBT.3

5. Which number is equal to three hundred four and two hundredths?

   A. 300.42
   B. 300.402
   C. 304.02
   D. 304.2

   5.NBT.3

6. Which statement below is true?

   A. 46.049 > 46.1
   B. 312.9 < 312.417
   C. 9.080 > 9.08
   D. 75.14 > 75.132

   5.NBT.3

TIP of the DAY

If you remember that when dividing by a power of 10 you should get a smaller number, you should be able to determine which direction to move the decimal point.

20

WEEK 2 : DAY 4

1. Which expression shows 30.21 in expanded form?

   A. $(3 \times 1) + \left(2 \times \frac{1}{1}\right) + \left(1 \times \frac{1}{10}\right)$

   B. $(3 \times 10) + \left(2 \times \frac{1}{1}\right) + \left(1 \times \frac{1}{10}\right)$

   C. $(3 \times 10) + \left(2 \times \frac{1}{10}\right) + \left(1 \times \frac{1}{100}\right)$

   D. $(3 \times 1) + \left(2 \times \frac{1}{10}\right) + \left(1 \times \frac{1}{100}\right)$

   5.NBT.3

2. $4(10{,}000) + 1(1{,}000) + 3(100) + 2(10) + 9(1) + 5\left(\frac{1}{10}\right) + 5\left(\frac{1}{100}\right)$

   Which number below is one-hundredth of the expanded form above?

   A. 413.2955
   B. 4132.955
   C. 41329.55
   D. 413295.5

   5.NBT.3

3. Which number below is the smallest?

   A. 412.261
   B. 412.19
   C. 412.04
   D. 412.038

   5.NBT.3

4. Which number is equal to five thousand twelve and sixty hundredths?

   A. 512.60
   B. 5012.60
   C. 5012.060
   D. 512,000.60

   5.NBT.3

5. Which expression shows 71.5 in expanded form?

   A. $(7 \times 1) + (1 \times 1) + \left(5 \times \frac{1}{10}\right)$

   B. $(7 \times 10) + (1 \times 1) + \left(5 \times \frac{1}{100}\right)$

   C. $(7 \times 10) + (1 \times 1) + \left(5 \times \frac{1}{10}\right)$

   D. $(7 \times 10) + (1 \times 1) + \left(5 \times \frac{1}{1}\right)$

   5.NBT.3

6. Which number below is the largest?

   A. 58.135
   B. 58.6
   C. 58.59
   D. 58.486

   5.NBT.3

TIP of the DAY

The word "and" means the whole numbers are finished and you're moving onto decimal numbers. Four and five tenths is 4 and $\frac{5}{10}$ or 4.5.

WEEK 2 : DAY 5

ASSESSMENT

1. Look at 764.51. In a different number, the 4 represents a value which is one-tenth of the value of the 4 in 764.51. What value is represented by the 4 in the other number?

   A. four hundredths
   B. four tenths
   C. four ones
   D. four tens

   5.NBT.1

2. $(8 \times 10{,}000) + (4 \times 1{,}000) + (7 \times 10) + (5 \times 1) + 3 \times \left(\dfrac{1}{100}\right)$

   Which number below is one-tenth of the expanded form above?

   A. 8,407.503
   B. 840.7503
   C. 84.07503
   D. 8.407503

   5.NBT.1
   5.NBT.3

3. Which number is the smallest?

   A. 817.9
   B. 871.003
   C. 817.1
   D. 817.099

   5.NBT.3

4. Which number sentence below is true?

   A. $(1 \times 100) + (6 \times 10) + (4 \times 1) + \left(3 \times \dfrac{1}{10}\right) > (1 \times 100) + (6 \times 10) + (4 \times 1) + \left(4 \times \dfrac{1}{100}\right)$

   B. $3.098 = (3 \times 1) + \left(9 \times \dfrac{1}{10}\right) + \left(8 \times \dfrac{1}{100}\right)$

   C. four hundredths > two tenths

   D. $(3 \times 10) + (4 \times 1) + \left(6 \times \dfrac{1}{10}\right) + \left(7 \times \dfrac{1}{100}\right) > 346.7$

   5.NBT.3

5. Which number is equal to fifty-five thousand and six hundredths?

   A. 55,600
   B. 55,000.6
   C. 55,000.06
   D. 505,000.06

   5.NBT.3

DAY 6 Challenge question

Write 245.016 in expanded form.

5.NBT.3

WEEK 3

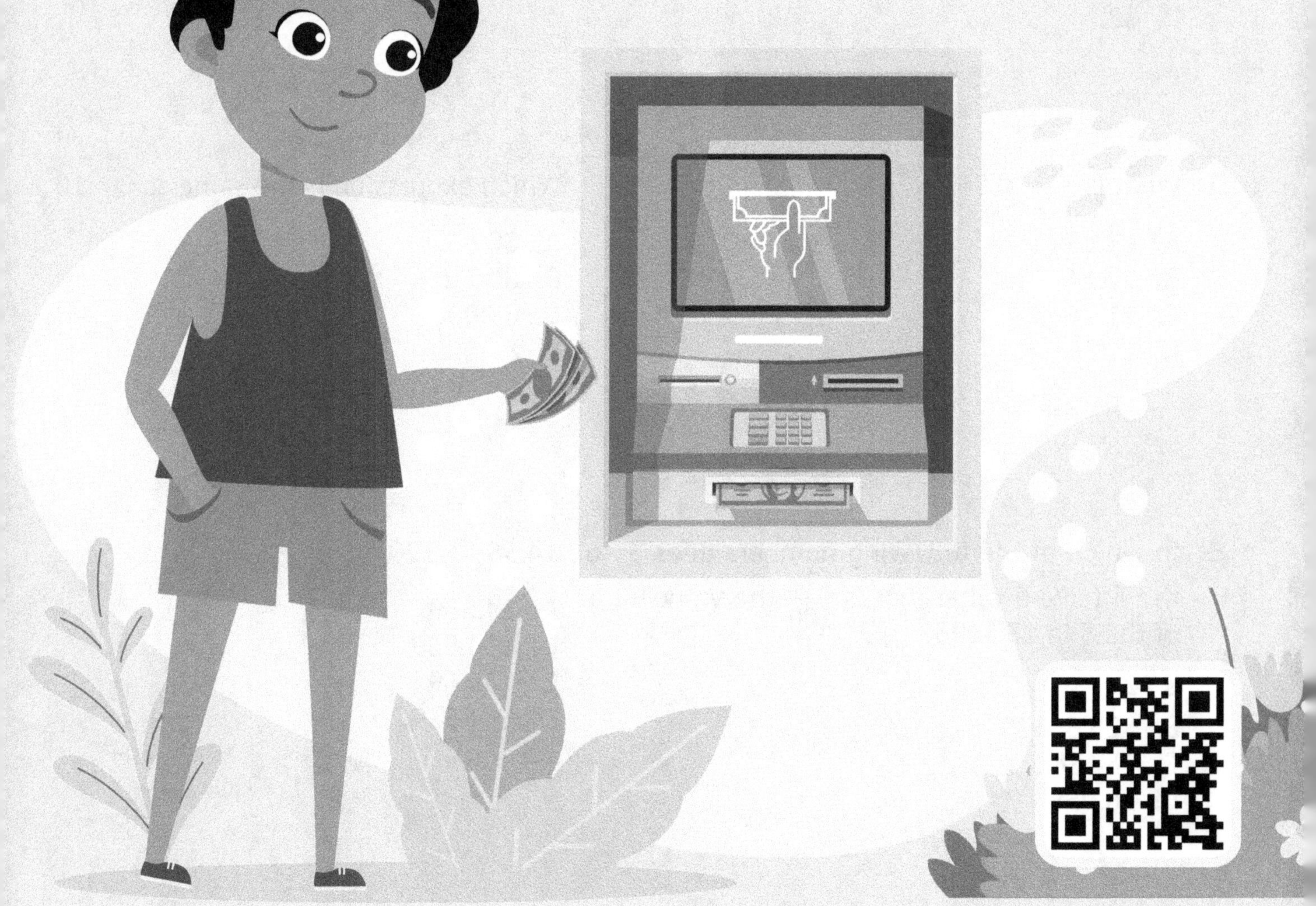

Week 3 will allow you to practice rounding numbers, even decimal numbers! You will also use multiplication for many of the questions.

You can find detailed video explanations of each problem in the book by visiting: ArgoPrep.com

WEEK 3 : DAY 1

1. Gas was $2.6894 per gallon. Round $2.6894 to the nearest hundredth.

   A. $2.6890
   B. $2.689
   C. $2.69
   D. $2.7

   5.NBT.4

2. What is 12 − 0.86?

   A. 12.86
   B. 12.14
   C. 11.14
   D. 11.86

   5.NBT.4

3. In which of the following numbers does the 5 have a value that is $\frac{1}{100}$ the value of the 5 in 13.5193?

   A. 4.105
   B. 529.3612
   C. 157.342
   D. 16.058

   5.NBT.1

4. Round 146.389 to the nearest hundred.

   A. 146.39
   B. 146.4
   C. 150
   D. 100

   5.NBT.4

5. Which expression is the same as 8×10^3?

   A. 80
   B. 800
   C. 8,000
   D. 80,000

   5.NBT.2

6. 14.569 + 120 = ?

   A. 14.689
   B. 134.569
   C. 135.69
   D. 144.569

   5.NBT.4

TIP of the DAY

For rounding, look at the digit to the right of the place you are rounding to.

24

WEEK 3 : DAY 2

The table below shows the lengths of 4 straws in millimeters. Use the table to answer questions 1 – 3.

Straw A	151.896
Straw B	152.3
Straw C	151.9
Straw D	152.47

1. Which statement about the straws is true?

    A. A > C
    B. B < D
    C. A > B
    D. D < C

    5.NBT.4

2. Which straw is the longest?

    A. A
    B. B
    C. C
    D. D

    5.NBT.3

3. Which statement about the straws is true?

    A. Straw B can round to 152.
    B. Straw D can round to 153.
    C. Straw C < Straw A
    D. Straw C is the shortest straw.

    5.NBT.4

4. What is 13,580.4729 rounded to the nearest thousandth?

    A. 13,580.472
    B. 13,580.473
    C. 13,000
    D. 14,000

    5.NBT.4

5. Which expression is equivalent to 1,000,000?

    A. 10^4
    B. 10^5
    C. 10^6
    D. 10^7

    5.NBT.2

Recall that a whole number like 14 has a decimal point after the 4 and can be written as 14 = 14.0.

WEEK 3 : DAY 3

1. Find the product of 12 and 68.

   A. 796
   B. 816
   C. 826
   D. 916

   5.NBT.5

2. What is 3,187 × 16?

   A. 5,992
   B. 47,805
   C. 50,976
   D. 50,992

   5.NBT.3
   5.NBT.4

The table below shows the cost of some items. Use it to answer questions 3 – 5.

Used car	$8,995
Refrigerator	$1,876
Couch	$568

3. What would be the cost of 8 cars?

   A. $61,960
   B. $62,965
   C. $71,960
   D. $80,955

   5.NBT.3

4. How much would 15 couches cost?

   A. $7,952
   B. $8,520
   C. $9,088
   D. $9,120

   5.NBT.5

5. What would be the cost of 10 refrigerators?

   A. $18,160
   B. $18,460
   C. $18,760
   D. $19,760

   5.NBT.5

TIP of the DAY

When multiplying by a power of 10, the decimal moves to the right the same number of places as there are zeroes in the power of 10.
Ex. 5×10^3 moves the decimal point 3 spaces to the right, so that the answer is 5,000

WEEK 3 : DAY 4

1. What is the product of 4,902 and 112?

   A. 54,924
   B. 55,104
   C. 533,022
   D. 549,024

   5.NBT.5

2. What is 365.17 + 429?

   A. 369.46
   B. 794.17
   C. 797.17
   D. 36,946

   5.NBT.4

3. The digit 3 in 57,831 is _____ times the value of the 3 in 13,650.

   A. 10
   B. 100
   C. $\frac{1}{10}$
   D. $\frac{1}{100}$

   5.NBT.1

4. Find: 3,068 × 205

   A. 9,200
   B. 75,440
   C. 628,940
   D. 76,700

   5.NBT.5

5. What is 7183.06 divided by 10^2?

   A. 7.18306
   B. 71.8306
   C. 718.306
   D. 718,306

   5.NBT.2

Tomorrow when you take the assessment, be careful to locate where each decimal point is in each number.

WEEK 3 : DAY 5

ASSESSMENT

1. What is the sum of 692.08 and 74?

   A. 692.82
   B. 699.48
   C. 766.08
   D. 1,432.08

   5.NBT.4

2. What is 47,861.593 rounded to the nearest tenth?

   A. 47,861.59
   B. 47,861.6
   C. 47,860
   D. 47,862

   5.NBT.4

3. What is 2,541.7891 rounded to the nearest thousandth?

   A. 2,541.789
   B. 2,541.79
   C. 2,541.8
   D. 2,540

   5.NBT.4

4. What is the product of 1,286 and 100?

   A. 12.86
   B. 128.6
   C. 12,860
   D. 128,600

   5.NBT.2

5. Which expression shows 47.05 in expanded form?

   A. $(4 \times 100) + (7 \times 10) + \left(5 \times \frac{1}{100}\right)$
   B. $(4 \times 10) + (7 \times 1) + \left(5 \times \frac{1}{10}\right)$
   C. $(4 \times 10) + (7 \times 1) + \left(5 \times \frac{1}{100}\right)$
   D. $(4 \times 10) + (7 \times 10) + \left(5 \times \frac{1}{10}\right)$

   5.NBT.3

6. What is 2,108 × 79?

   A. 17,222
   B. 164,342
   C. 166,532
   D. 168,722

   5.NBT.5

DAY 6
Challenge question

Find 92 + 16.83. Take that sum and multiply by 10^3. What number do you get?

5.NBT.2/5.NBT.4

WEEK 4

VIDEO EXPLANATIONS — ARGOPREP.COM

Week 4 has lots of decimals. Be sure to line up the decimals when adding or subtracting and count decimals when multiplying.

You can find detailed video explanations of each problem in the book by visiting: ArgoPrep.com

WEEK 4 : DAY 1

1. Which equation is shown in the model below?

   A. 30 ÷ 6 = 5   C. 24 ÷ 6 = 5
   B. 25 ÷ 5 = 5   D. 30 ÷ 5 = 5

   5.NBT.6

2. What is the quotient when 1,620 is divided by 12?

   A. 125   C. 145
   B. 135   D. 205

   5.NBT.6

3. Find: 6300 ÷ 36 = ?

   A. 155   C. 175
   B. 165   D. 185

   5.NBT.6

4. What is the value of the expression below?

   7056 ÷ 18

   A. 385   C. 395
   B. 392   D. 402

   5.NBT.6

5. How many times greater is the value of the digit 7 in 175,059 than the value of the digit 7 in 839,725?

   A. 10 times
   B. 100 times
   C. 1,000 times
   D. 10,000 times

   5.NBT.1

6. Which relationship could be shown by the model below?

   A. 84 × 14 = 6
   B. 14 ÷ 6 = 84
   C. 84 × 6 = 14
   D. 84 ÷ 14 = 6

   5.NBT.6

TIP of the DAY

You have completed more than 3 weeks worth of work – great job!

WEEK 4 : DAY 2

1. There are 11 shelves that contain a total of 5,676 rolls of tape. How many rolls are on each shelf?

   A. 56
   B. 506
   C. 516
   D. 526

   5.NBT.6

2. What is the value of the expression below?

   $$4050 \div 45$$

   A. 90
   B. 99
   C. 900
   D. 909

   5.NBT.6

3. Which equation is NOT shown in the model below?

   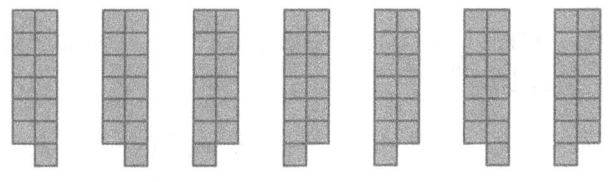

   A. 13 × 7 = 91
   B. 7 × 13 = 91
   C. 91 ÷ 13 = 7
   D. 13 + 7 = 91

   5.NBT.6

4. Look at 415.82. In a different number, the 4 represents a value which is one-tenth of the value of the 4 in 415.82. What value is represented by the 4 in the other number?

   A. four hundredths
   B. four tenths
   C. four ones
   D. four tens

   5.NBT.1

5. What is the value of the expression below?

   $$2376 \div 22$$

   A. 18
   B. 80
   C. 108
   D. 180

   5.NBT.6

6. Abby knocked down 3,252 pins in 12 games. How many pins did she knock per game?

   A. 217
   B. 271
   C. 291
   D. 317

   5.NBT.6

TIP of the DAY

You can check your answers by rounding the numbers in the original problem to see if your answers are reasonable.

WEEK 4 : DAY 3

1. What is 6,050 divided by 25?

   A. 24
   B. 242
   C. 245
   D. 2042

   5.NBT.6

2. What is the value of the expression below?

   $$12.08 + 69.3$$

   A. 21.71
   B. 41.71
   C. 81.38
   D. 813.8

   5.NBT.7

3. What is the value of the expression below?

   $$62.04 \times 9.1$$

   A. 56.456
   B. 564.26
   C. 564.564
   D. 567.84

   5.NBT.7

4. Which term can be put in the blank to make the statement true?

   $$940{,}000 = 94 \text{ _____}$$

   A. thousands
   B. ten-thousands
   C. hundred-thousands
   D. millions

   5.NBT.1

5. What is the value of the expression below?

   $$57.6 \div 1.5$$

   A. 38.4
   B. 39.4
   C. 39.3
   D. 40.3

   5.NBT.7

6. What is the value of the expression below?

   $$1{,}256 - 316.52$$

   A. 303.96
   B. 323.48
   C. 938.48
   D. 939.48

   5.NBT.7

TIP of the DAY

When adding or subtracting numbers that contain decimals, be sure to line up the decimals before performing the addition or subtraction.

WEEK 4 : DAY 4

1. Which statement is NOT true about the expression below?

   980.6 + 213.54

   A. 980.6 + 213.54 does not equal 767.06.
   B. 767.06 is not the answer because the sum should be around 1200.
   C. 3116.0 is not the answer because there should be 2 numbers to the right of the decimal point.
   D. 3116.0 is the answer.

   5.NBT.7

2. Alex bought some Halloween candy. One large bag cost $18.98, a medium bag cost $12.54 and the third bag cost $9. How much did Alex spend on candy?

   A. $31.52
   B. $31.61
   C. $40.52
   D. $41.61

   5.NBT.7

3. Ally had 26.8 gallons of gas in her car. She used up 14.9 gallons. How many gallons remain in her car?

   A. 11.1
   B. 11.9
   C. 41.1
   D. 41.7

   5.NBT.7

4. What is the value of the expression below?

   1318.4 ÷ 32

   A. 41.2
   B. 41.8
   C. 42.2
   D. 42.8

   5.NBT.7

5. In which of the following numbers does the 2 have a value that is 100 times the value of the 2 in 8,054,276?

   A. 9,362,451
   B. 7,649,672
   C. 3,108,624
   D. 7,820,356

   5.NBT.1

6. Which expression shows 8643.7 in expanded form?

   A. $(8 \times 1000) + (6 \times 10) + (4 \times 10) + (3 \times 1) + \left(7 \times \frac{1}{10}\right)$
   B. $(8 \times 1000) + (6 \times 100) + (4 \times 10) + (3 \times 1) + \left(7 \times \frac{1}{100}\right)$
   C. $(8 \times 1000) + (6 \times 100) + (4 \times 10) + (3 \times 1) + \left(7 \times \frac{1}{10}\right)$
   D. $(8 \times 10,000) + (6 \times 1000) + (4 \times 10) + (3 \times 1) + \left(7 \times \frac{1}{100}\right)$

   5.NBT.3

TIP of the DAY

When working on word problems, be sure to know what operation to use. Do you add, subtract, multiply or divide?

WEEK 4 : DAY 5

ASSESSMENT

1. What is the value of the expression below?

   3313.9 ÷ 31

   A. 16.9
   B. 106.9
   C. 160.9
   D. 169.0

   5.NBT.7

2. Andrew had 5,144 pounds of sand that he had to spread over 16 driveways. How much sand should each driveway get?

   A. 231.5 pounds
   B. 281.5 pounds
   C. 321.5 pounds
   D. 381.5 pounds

   5.NBT.6

3. What is the value of the expression below?

   138.4 × 8.2

   A. 1,134.88
   B. 11,348.0
   C. 11,348.8
   D. 113,488

   5.NBT.7

4. If Asa split 5,436 golf balls among 9 players, how many golf balls did each player receive?

   A. 64   C. 74
   B. 604   D. 704

   5.NBT.6

5. Annie had 40 meters of rope to outline the beach volleyball court. If she needed 56.3 meters, how many more meters of rope did Annie need?

   A. 96.7   C. 16.7
   B. 96.3   D. 16.3

   5.NBT.7

6. Which expression shows 709.02 in expanded form?

   A. $(7 \times 100) + (9 \times 1) + \left(2 \times \frac{1}{10}\right)$

   B. $(7 \times 100) + (9 \times 10) + \left(2 \times \frac{1}{100}\right)$

   C. $(7 \times 10) + (9 \times 1) + \left(2 \times \frac{1}{100}\right)$

   D. $(7 \times 100) + (9 \times 1) + \left(2 \times \frac{1}{100}\right)$

   5.NBT.3

DAY 6 Challenge question

Write an equation that can be used to find the answer to 125.07 − 37.918.

5.NBT.7

WEEK 5

VIDEO EXPLANATIONS

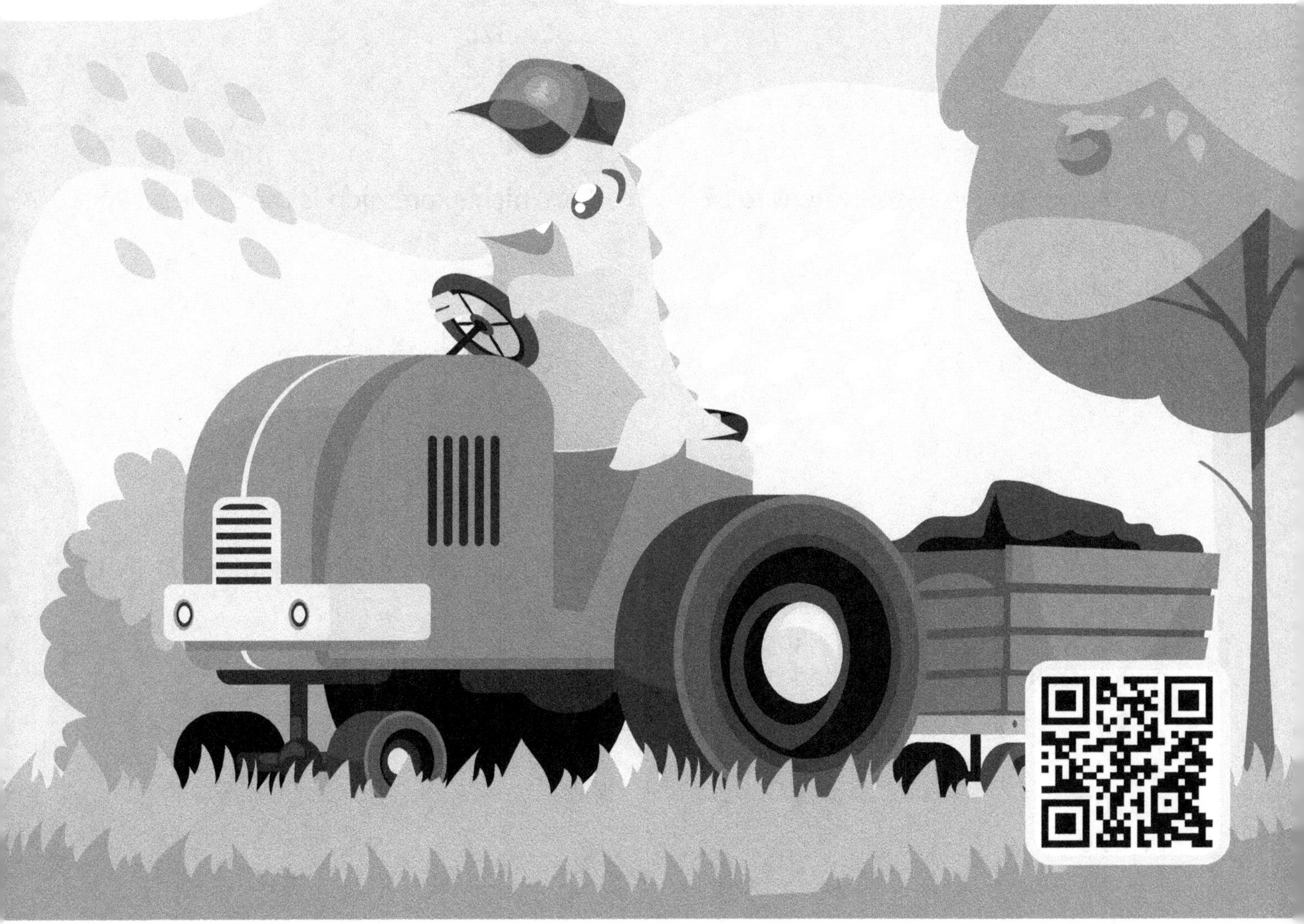

This week you will be able to try taking English phrases and turning them into math problems. Week 5 also practices recognizing how two different patterns compare to each other.

You can find detailed video explanations of each problem in the book by visiting: ArgoPrep.com

WEEK 5 : DAY 1

1. What is the value of the expression below?

    $$[36 - (8 \times 2) + 10] \div 5$$

    A. 0
    B. 4
    C. 5
    D. 6

    5.OA.1

2. Which expression is equivalent to 8?

    A. $(4 \times 6) \div 3$
    B. $3 \times (2 \times 6) \div 3$
    C. $(4 \times 4) - 6$
    D. $2 + (4 + 6) \div 2$

    5.OA.1

3. Brianne had 1,284 kilograms of mulch that she needed to spread over 12 flowerbeds. How many kilograms of mulch should each flowerbed get?

    A. 17
    B. 97
    C. 107
    D. 170

    5.NBT.6

4. What is the value of the expression below?

    $$3 \times [26 + 5(3 \times 2) - 10]$$

    A. 46
    B. 138
    C. 528
    D. 488

    5.OA.1

5. Which expression is the same as 9×10^4?

    A. 90
    B. 900
    C. 9,000
    D. 90,000

    5.NBT.2

6. Which expression is equivalent to 10?

    A. $(4 \times 6) \div 3$
    B. $3 \times (2 \times 6) \div 3$
    C. $(4 \times 4) - 6$
    D. $2 + (4 + 6) \div 2$

    5.OA.1

Remember to do multiplication and division before addition and subtraction when there are no parentheses.

WEEK 5 : DAY 2

1. What is the value of the expression below?

   12 + [8 × (5 × 2) − 20] ÷ 4

   A. 18
   B. 27
   C. 45
   D. 60

   5.OA.1

2. Which expression is equivalent to 45?

   A. 100 − (9 × 6)
   B. (8 + 6) × 3
   C. 75 − 6 × 5
   D. 2 × (8 + 3) × 2

   5.OA.1

3. What is the value of the expression below?

   25 − [5 + (1 × 2) + 3] ÷ 5

   A. 2
   B. 3
   C. 13
   D. 23

   5.OA.1

4. Which expression is equivalent to 66?

   A. 39 - (6 × 6) ÷ 3
   B. 25 - 3 × 3
   C. (8 × 9) - 6
   D. 3 × (4 + 6) × 2

   5.OA.1

5. What is 5685 + 842.91?

   A. 4842.09
   B. 5842.91
   C. 6527.91
   D. 6697.91

   5.NBT.4

6. What is 4213.715 rounded to the nearest thousandth?

   A. 4000
   B. 4213.715
   C. 4213.72
   D. 4213.7

   5.NBT.4

TIP of the DAY: *Complete grouping symbols (parentheses, brackets, braces) before computing multiplication and division.*

WEEK 5 : DAY 3

1. Which expression is equivalent to 49?

    A. (64 − 16) + 3 ÷ 3
    B. (18 − 3) × 3 + 1
    C. 4 + 3 × 7
    D. 8 + (12 − 2 × 2) + 13

    5.OA.1

2. What is the value of the expression below?

    [36 − (3 × 4) + 6] + 10 ÷ 5

    A. 8
    B. 30
    C. 32
    D. 45

    5.OA.1

3. What is the value of the expression below?

    1300 ÷ 1.3

    A. 1
    B. 10
    C. 100
    D. 1,000

    5.NBT.7

4. What is the product of 5016 and 32?

    A. 155,496
    B. 158,432
    C. 160,480
    D. 160,512

    5.NBT.5

5. What is the value of the expression below?

    15 + (45 ÷ 5) × 4

    A. 48
    B. 51
    C. 96
    D. 220

    5.OA.1

6. What is the value of the expression below?

    7 × 3 + (20 − 12) × 4

    A. 45
    B. 53
    C. 108
    D. 116

    5.OA.1

Be sure to use the correct order of operations. If not, you may end up with a completely different answer.

WEEK 5 : DAY 4

1. Which statement is true about the values of the two expressions below?

   Expression A: 5 × (23 − 18)
   Expression B: 23 − 18

   A. The value of Expression A is 5 times the value of Expression B.
   B. The value of Expression B is 5 times the value of Expression A.
   C. The value of Expression A is 5 more than the value of Expression B.
   D. The value of Expression B is 5 more than the value of Expression A.

   5.OA.2

4. Which statement is true about the values of the two expressions below?

   Expression A: (3 × 9)
   Expression B: (3 × 9) + 7

   A. The value of Expression A is 7 times the value of Expression B.
   B. The value of Expression B is 7 times the value of Expression A.
   C. The value of Expression A is 7 more than the value of Expression B.
   D. The value of Expression B is 7 more than the value of Expression A.

   5.OA.2

2. Which mathematical expression is equivalent to the number sentence below?

   Add 18 to 24, and then multiply by 6.

   A. 24 + 18 × 6   C. 24 + (18 × 6)
   B. 18 + (24 × 6)   D. (24 + 18) × 6

   5.OA.2

5. Which mathematical expression is equivalent to the number sentence below?

   Triple the sum of 11 and 24.

   A. 2 × (11 + 24)   C. 3 × (11 + 24)
   B. 3 × 11 + 24   D. (3 × 11) + 24

   5.OA.2

3. Which number in standard form is equivalent to the number below?

   $(6 \times 1000) + (8 \times 100) + (5 \times 10) + (3 \times 1) + \left(9 \times \frac{1}{100}\right)$

   A. 6,853.9   C. 6,583.09
   B. 6,853.09   D. 6,853.009

   5.NBT.3

6. The digit 5 in 40,675 is _____ times the value of the 5 in 71,350.

   A. 10   C. $\frac{1}{10}$
   B. 100   D. $\frac{1}{100}$

   5.NBT.1

Tip of the Day: Pay close attention to phrasing. Parentheses, commas and order can affect the meanings of the expressions.

WEEK 5 : DAY 5

ASSESSMENT

1. What is the value of the expression below?

    $$100 - [(4 \times 6) + 20] \div 4$$

    A. 81
    B. 89
    C. 149
    D. 581

    5.OA.1

2. Which expression is equivalent to 63?

    A. $12 \times 4 + 3 \times 5$
    B. $(3 + 5) \times 12 \div 3$
    C. $16 - 3 \times 4 + 11$
    D. $7 \times (8 + 7)$

    5.OA.1

3. Which mathematical expression is equivalent to the number sentence below?

    The sum of 12 and 13 is divided by 5.

    A. $12 + 13 \div 5$
    B. $(12 + 13) \div 5$
    C. $(13 - 12) \div 5$
    D. $(12 \times 13) \div 5$

    5.OA.2

4. Which statement is true about the values of the two expressions below?

    Expression A: $(21 \times 16) - 10$
    Expression B: (21×16)

    A. The value of Expression A is 10 times the value of Expression B.
    B. The value of Expression B is 10 times the value of Expression A.
    C. The value of Expression A is 10 less than the value of Expression B.
    D. The value of Expression B is 10 less than the value of Expression A.

    5.OA.2

5. What is the product of 6.08 and 1000?

    A. 6.08000   C. 608
    B. 60.8   D. 6080

    5.NBT.2

6. Which expression shows 186.4 in expanded form?

    A. $(1 \times 100) + (8 \times 10) + (6 \times 1) + \left(4 \times \frac{1}{10}\right)$
    B. $(1 \times 1000) + (8 \times 10) + (6 \times 1) + \left(4 \times \frac{1}{10}\right)$
    C. $(1 \times 1000) + (8 \times 10) + (6 \times 1) + \left(4 \times \frac{1}{100}\right)$
    D. $(1 \times 100) + (8 \times 10) + (6 \times 1) + \left(4 \times \frac{1}{100}\right)$

    5.NBT.3

DAY 6 Challenge question

Write a number sentence for the phrase "twelve less than the product of seven and five".

5.OA.2

WEEK 6

During Week 6, you will have more opportunities to develop the skills needed to compare number patterns and even to create your own number patterns.

You can find detailed video explanations of each problem in the book by visiting: ArgoPrep.com

WEEK 6 : DAY 1

1. Which expression represents the phrase "eight less than the product of three and six"?

   A. (3 × 6) – 8
   B. 8 – (3 × 6)
   C. (3 + 6) – 8
   D. 8 – (3 + 6)

   5.OA.2

2. Which statement is true about the values of the two expressions below?

   Expression A: 2 × (9 + 4)
   Expression B: (9 + 4)

   A. The value of Expression A is twice the value of Expression B.
   B. The value of Expression B is twice the value of Expression A.
   C. The value of Expression A is 2 more than the value of Expression B.
   D. The value of Expression B is 2 more than the value of Expression A.

   5.OA.2

3. Which mathematical expression is equivalent to the number sentence below?

   Four more than the product of fifteen and three.

   A. (15 × 3) + 4
   B. (15 ÷ 3) + 4
   C. (15 + 3) + 4
   D. (15 – 3) + 4

   5.OA.2

4. Which expression represents the phrase "nine more than the quotient of 75 and 5"?

   A. 75 ÷ (5 + 9)
   B. 75 ÷ 5 + 9
   C. 75 × 5 + 9
   D. (75 × 5) + 9

   5.OA.2

5. Which statement is true about the values of the two expressions below?

   Expression A: (8 × 11) – 6
   Expression B: (8 × 11)

   A. The value of Expression A is six times the value of Expression B.
   B. The value of Expression B is six times the value of Expression A.
   C. The value of Expression A is 6 more than the value of Expression B.
   D. The value of Expression B is 6 more than the value of Expression A.

   5.OA.2

6. In which of the following numbers does the 3 have a value that is $\frac{1}{10}$ the value of the 3 in 453,261?

   A. 2,362,510
   B. 4,639,578
   C. 6,173,624
   D. 1,820,366

   5.NBT.1

TIP of the DAY

Sometimes when a phrase says "6 less than 8" you may want to write 6 – 8. This is incorrect, it would be 8 – 6.

42

WEEK 6 : DAY 2

1. Which phrase best matches the expression below?

   3 × (15 − 8)

   A. Three more than the difference between 15 and 8
   B. Three less than the difference between 15 and 8
   C. Three times the difference between 15 and 8
   D. Three times the quotient of 15 and 8

   5.OA.2

2. Which expression is equivalent to 32?

   A. 12 × 4 − 3 × 5
   B. (3 + 5) × 12 ÷ 3
   C. 16 − 3 × 4 + 11
   D. 4 × (7 + 4)

   5.OA.1

3. Which statement is true about the values of the two expressions below?

   Expression A: (18 + 13)
   Expression B: 2 × (18 + 13)

   A. The value of Expression A is half the value of Expression B.
   B. The value of Expression B is half the value of Expression A.
   C. The value of Expression A is 2 less than the value of Expression B.
   D. The value of Expression B is 2 less than the value of Expression A.

   5.OA.2

4. Which mathematical expression is equivalent to the number sentence below?

   Double the difference between 13 and 6.

   A. 2 × 13 − 6   C. (2 × 13) − 6
   B. 13 − 6 × 2   D. 2 × (13 − 6)

   5.OA.2

5. They paid $26.75 for pizza, $12 for drinks, and $7.41 for a tip. How much did the entire meal cost?

   A. $34.28   C. $46.16
   B. $44.16   D. $49.28

   5.NBT.7

6. Which expression shows 791.08 in expanded form?

   A. $(7 \times 100) + (9 \times 10) + (1 \times 10) + \left(8 \times \frac{1}{10}\right)$

   B. $(7 \times 100) + (9 \times 10) + (1 \times 1) + \left(8 \times \frac{1}{100}\right)$

   C. $(7 \times 1000) + (9 \times 10) + (1 \times 1) + \left(8 \times \frac{1}{10}\right)$

   D. $(7 \times 100) + (9 \times 100) + (1 \times 1) + \left(8 \times \frac{1}{100}\right)$

   5.NBT.3

TIP of the DAY

Sometimes if you are working on math for a long time, it is a good idea to take a little break to allow your brain to rest. Take a walk, read a book, or just go outside for a bit.

WEEK 6 : DAY 3

1. Which phrase best matches the expression below?

   (5 × 7) – 9

   A. Nine more than the product of five and seven
   B. Nine less than the product of five and seven
   C. Nine less than the quotient of five and seven
   D. Nine more than the quotient of five and seven

   5.OA.2

2. There are two number patterns below.

   Pattern I: 0, 4, 8, 12, ...
   Pattern II: 0, 3, 6, 9, ...

   Which statement is true about the patterns?

   A. All of the numbers in the 2 patterns are different.
   B. All of the numbers in Pattern I are 1 more than the numbers in Pattern II.
   C. The sixth number in Pattern II is larger than the fourth number in Pattern I.
   D. The fifth number in Pattern I is equal to the sixth number in Pattern II.

   5.OA.3

The table below shows the cost of several gallons of gas. Use the table to answer questions 3 – 5.

Gallons of Gas	Cost (dollars)
2	6
4	12
6	18

3. What is the cost for 3 gallons of gas?

   A. $3   C. $9
   B. $6   D. $12

   5.OA.3

4. Which statement is true about the table above?

   A. The cost is always three times the number of gallons.
   B. Five gallons of gas would cost $14.
   C. One gallon of gas would be $1.50.
   D. The cost is always double the number of gallons.

   5.OA.3

5. What would you expect the cost of 10 gallons of gas to be?

   A. $21   C. $27
   B. $24   D. $30

   5.OA.3

TIP of the DAY

Patterns are consistent. They are like "rules" that numbers follow.

WEEK 6 : DAY 4

1. There are two number patterns below.

    Pattern I: 0, 2, 4, 6, ...
    Pattern II: 0, 3, 6, 9, ...

    Which statement is true about the patterns?

    A. All of the numbers in the Pattern I are also in Pattern II.
    B. All of the numbers in Pattern I are even numbers.
    C. All of the numbers in Pattern II are odd numbers.
    D. The fifth number in Pattern I is more than the fifth number in Pattern II.

    5.OA.3

The graph below shows the number of grapes Bella ate per day. Days are on the horizontal x-axis and the number of grapes eaten are on the vertical y-axis. Use the graph below to answer questions 2 – 4.

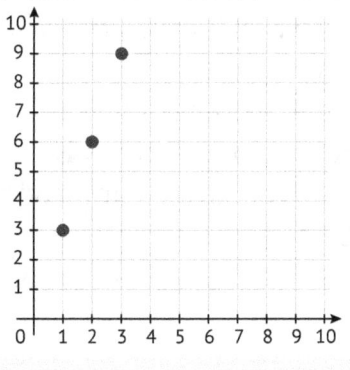

2. On what day did Bella eat 9 grapes?

    A. Day 1
    B. Day 2
    C. Day 3
    D. Day 4

    5.OA.3

3. How many grapes would Bella eat on Day 5?

    A. 12
    B. 15
    C. 18
    D. 21

    5.OA.3

4. Which statement is true about the graph?

    A. Bella eats 3 grapes per day.
    B. The number of grapes is double whatever number day it is.
    C. On Day 8 Bella will eat 11 grapes.
    D. Each day Bella eats 3 more grapes than the day before.

    5.OA.3

5. Look at 865.21. In a different number, the 5 represents a value which is one-tenth of the value of the 5 in 865.21. What value is represented by the 5 in the other number?

    A. five hundredths
    B. five tenths
    C. five ones
    D. five tens

    5.NBT.1

You are really close to completing another week. Keep working hard!

45

WEEK 6 : DAY 5

ASSESSMENT

1. There are two number patterns below.

    Pattern A: 0, 5, 10, 15, …
    Pattern B: 0, 2, 4, 6, …

    Which statement is true about the patterns?

    A. None of the numbers in Pattern B are in Pattern A.
    B. All of the numbers in Pattern B are odd numbers.
    C. All of the numbers in Pattern A are even numbers.
    D. Pattern A is increasing more than twice as fast as Pattern B.

    5.OA.3

3. Which statement is true about the chart?

    A. The days are increasing in number slower than the temperature is increasing in degrees.
    B. Day 4 would likely have a change in temperature of 15 degrees.
    C. The temperature would change 28 degrees on Day 6.
    D. The Temperature numbers are triple the Day numbers.

    5.OA.3

The chart below shows the change in temperature on certain days. Use the chart to answer questions 2 – 3.

Day	Temperature (°F)
1	4
2	8
3	12

2. What would you expect to be the amount of change on Day 5?

    A. 15 degrees
    B. 16 degrees
    C. 20 degrees
    D. 24 degrees

    5.OA.3

4. There are two number patterns below.

    Pattern A: 0, 2, 4, 6, …
    Pattern B: 0, 1, 2, 3, …

    Which statement is true about the patterns?

    A. Pattern B is increasing twice as fast as Pattern A.
    B. There are no numbers that are in both Pattern A and Pattern B.
    C. Pattern A is increasing twice as fast as Pattern B.
    D. Pattern B has only even numbers.

    5.OA.3

DAY 6
Challenge question

Write 2 expressions that mean "two more than the product of twelve and three".

5.OA.2

WEEK 7

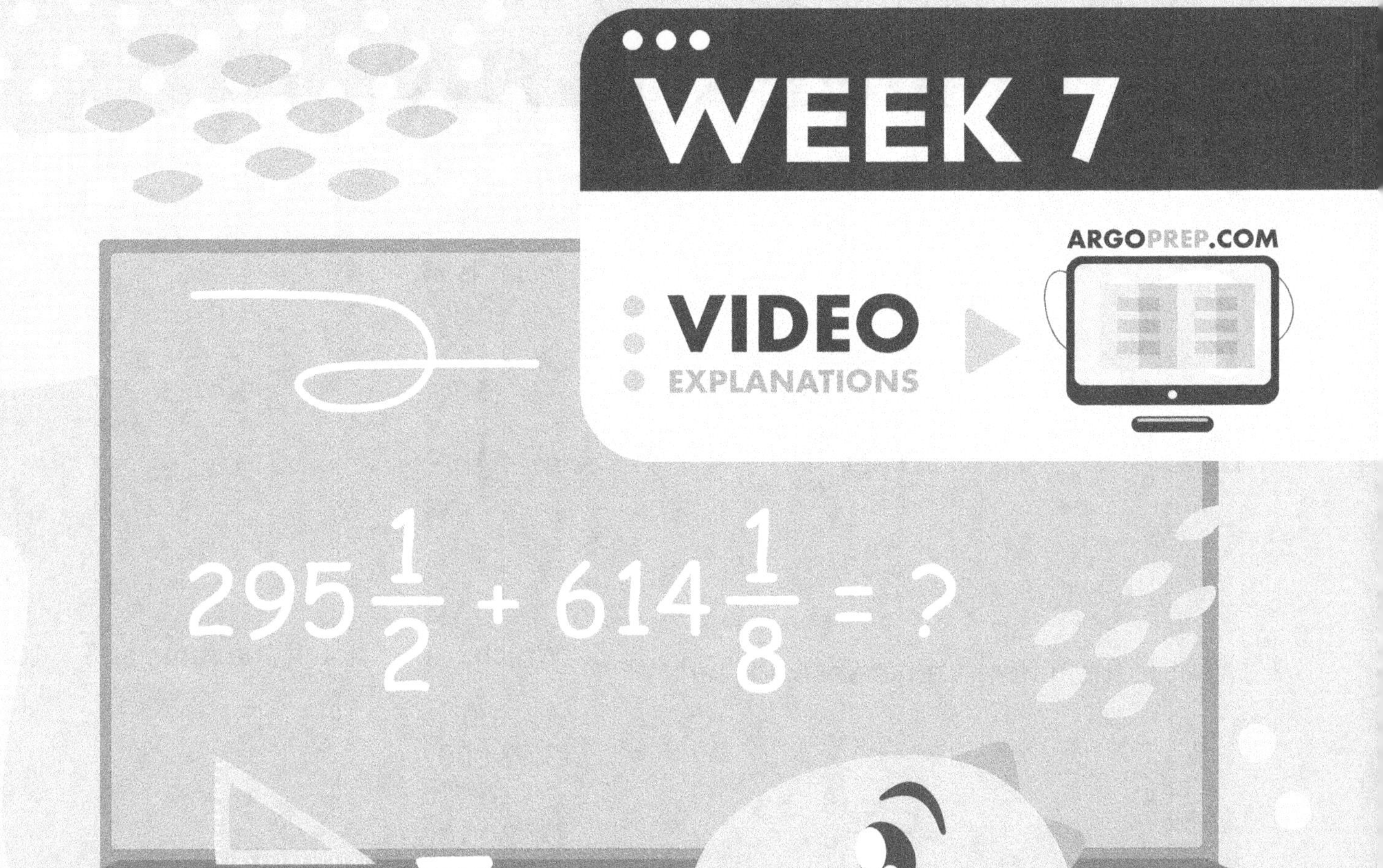

$$295\frac{1}{2} + 614\frac{1}{8} = ?$$

Now that you've mastered decimal calculations, Week 7 will give you practice working with fractions. Do well!

You can find detailed video explanations of each problem in the book by visiting: ArgoPrep.com

WEEK 7 : DAY 1

1. $5\frac{4}{5} + 18\frac{1}{4} = ?$

   A. $23\frac{1}{20}$
   B. $23\frac{5}{9}$
   C. $24\frac{1}{20}$
   D. $24\frac{5}{9}$

   5.NF.1

2. What is the difference between $49\frac{8}{9}$ and $17\frac{1}{3}$?

   A. $32\frac{5}{9}$
   B. $32\frac{7}{12}$
   C. $33\frac{5}{9}$
   D. $33\frac{7}{9}$

   5.NF.1

3. Find: $\frac{3}{5} + \frac{1}{3}$

   A. $\frac{1}{2}$
   B. $\frac{4}{8}$
   C. $\frac{4}{15}$
   D. $\frac{14}{15}$

   5.NF.1

4. What is $28 - 24\frac{1}{3}$?

   A. $4\frac{2}{3}$
   B. $4\frac{1}{3}$
   C. $3\frac{2}{3}$
   D. $3\frac{1}{3}$

   5.NF.1

5. Which expression is the same as 3×10^5?

   A. 300
   B. 3,000
   C. 30,000
   D. 300,000

   5.NBT.2

6. Which expression is equivalent to 10?

   A. $(4 \times 6) \div 3$
   B. $3 \times (2 \times 6) \div 3$
   C. $(4 \times 4) - 6$
   D. $2 + (4 + 6) \div 2$

   5.OA.1

TIP of the DAY

Before adding or subtracting fractions, you need to make sure they have the same denominator.

WEEK 7 : DAY 2

1. $72\frac{1}{5} - 46\frac{2}{3} = ?$

   A. $25\frac{1}{2}$ C. $26\frac{1}{2}$

   B. $25\frac{8}{15}$ D. $26\frac{8}{15}$

   5.NF.1

2. What is the sum of 36 and $26\frac{5}{7}$?

   A. $9\frac{5}{7}$ C. $61\frac{5}{7}$

   B. $10\frac{5}{7}$ D. $62\frac{5}{7}$

   5.NF.1

3. Find: $\frac{8}{9} - \frac{1}{3}$

   A. $\frac{5}{9}$ C. $\frac{6}{7}$

   B. $\frac{2}{3}$ D. $\frac{7}{6}$

   5.NF.1

4. What is $8\frac{3}{4} + 7\frac{3}{8}$?

   A. $15\frac{6}{12}$ C. $15\frac{7}{8}$

   B. $15\frac{3}{4}$ D. $16\frac{1}{8}$

   5.NF.1

5. Which statement is true about the values of the two expressions below?

   Expression A: 12 + (13 × 82)
   Expression B: 13 × 82

   A. The value of Expression A is 12 times the value of Expression B.
   B. The value of Expression B is 12 times the value of Expression A.
   C. The value of Expression A is 12 more than the value of Expression B.
   D. The value of Expression B is 12 more than the value of Expression A.

   5.OA.2

6. What is 326.0798 rounded to the nearest tenth?

   A. 330   C. 326.08
   B. 326.1   D. 326.080

   5.NBT.4

TIP of the DAY

When subtracting a fraction or mixed number from a whole number, don't forget to subtract 1 from the whole number if you need to rename the fraction.

WEEK 7 : DAY 3

1. What is the difference between $19\frac{1}{7}$ and 8?

   A. $10\frac{1}{7}$ C. $11\frac{1}{7}$

   B. $10\frac{6}{7}$ D. $17\frac{1}{7}$

   5.NF.1

2. What is $12\frac{3}{4} + 17\frac{1}{2}$?

   A. $19\frac{4}{6}$ C. $29\frac{1}{4}$

   B. $25\frac{1}{2}$ D. $30\frac{1}{4}$

   5.NF.1

3. $19\frac{7}{8} + 23\frac{4}{5} = ?$

   A. $43\frac{27}{40}$ C. $42\frac{37}{40}$

   B. $43\frac{7}{10}$ D. $42\frac{7}{10}$

   5.NF.1

4. What is the product of 3,781 and 85?

   A. 311,905
   B. 319,485
   C. 321,105
   D. 321,385

   5.NBT.5

5. Find: $\frac{3}{8} + \frac{11}{12}$

   A. $\frac{7}{10}$ C. $1\frac{7}{24}$

   B. $\frac{14}{24}$ D. $1\frac{10}{24}$

   5.NF.1

6. What is $100 - 93\frac{8}{9}$?

   A. $6\frac{1}{9}$ C. $7\frac{1}{9}$

   B. $6\frac{8}{9}$ D. $7\frac{8}{9}$

   5.NF.1

TIP of the DAY

When adding fractions, if the sum is an improper fraction, remember to make it a mixed number and add the whole number to the other whole numbers.

WEEK 7 : DAY 4

1. What is $36\frac{3}{4} + 43\frac{4}{5}$?

   A. $79\frac{7}{9}$ C. $80\frac{11}{20}$

   B. $79\frac{11}{20}$ D. $81\frac{7}{9}$

   5.NF.1

2. Find: $41\frac{1}{3} - 8\frac{5}{6}$

   A. $32\frac{1}{2}$ C. $33\frac{1}{3}$

   B. $32\frac{2}{3}$ D. $33\frac{2}{3}$

   5.NF.1

3. What is the difference between $67\frac{1}{2}$ and $36\frac{2}{3}$?

   A. $31\frac{1}{6}$ C. $31\frac{5}{6}$

   B. $31\frac{1}{3}$ D. $30\frac{5}{6}$

   5.NF.1

4. Find: $\frac{2}{3} + \frac{3}{8} + \frac{1}{4}$

   A. $\frac{6}{15}$ C. $1\frac{5}{24}$

   B. $\frac{23}{24}$ D. $1\frac{7}{24}$

   5.NF.1

5. The digit 2 in 42,517 is _____ times the value of the 2 in 87,263.

   A. 10   C. $\frac{1}{10}$

   B. 100   D. $\frac{1}{100}$

   5.NBT.1

6. Which number in standard form is equivalent to the number below?

   $(3 \times 1{,}000) + (8 \times 100) + (4 \times 10) + (7 \times 1) + \left(1 \times \frac{1}{100}\right) + \left(2 \times \frac{1}{1000}\right)$

   A. 30,847.012
   B. 3,847.0012
   C. 3,847.012
   D. 3,847.12

   5.NBT.3

TIP of the DAY

Tomorrow when you take the assessment, please check your answers to see if they are reasonable.

51

WEEK 7 : DAY 5

ASSESSMENT

1. What is $78\frac{4}{5} - 36\frac{1}{3}$?

   A. $41\frac{5}{8}$ C. $42\frac{5}{8}$

   B. $41\frac{7}{15}$ D. $42\frac{7}{15}$

   5.NF.1

2. Find: $127\frac{1}{2} + 396\frac{3}{4}$

   A. $524\frac{4}{7}$ C. $424\frac{3}{4}$

   B. $524\frac{1}{4}$ D. $413\frac{1}{4}$

   5.NF.1

3. What is the difference between 100 and $56\frac{3}{8}$?

   A. $43\frac{3}{8}$ C. $44\frac{3}{8}$

   B. $43\frac{5}{8}$ D. $44\frac{5}{8}$

   5.NF.1

4. Use the chart below to answer the question.

Pattern A	Pattern B
2	6
3	9
4	12

   Which statement is true about the patterns shown in the table?

   A. Pattern B numbers are 4 more than the numbers in Pattern A.
   B. Pattern A is increasing faster than Pattern B.
   C. Pattern B numbers are 3 times the numbers in Pattern A.
   D. The numbers in Pattern A have $\frac{1}{2}$ the value as numbers in Pattern B.

   5.OA.3

5. What is the quotient of 312,950 and 1000?

   A. 312,950,000
   B. 3129.5
   C. 312.95
   D. 31.295

   5.NBT.2

DAY 6
Challenge question

Find the value of: $6\frac{2}{3} + 14\frac{3}{8} - 12\frac{3}{4}$

5.NF.1

52

WEEK 8

VIDEO EXPLANATIONS — ARGOPREP.COM

You will get additional practice with fractions during Week 8. You will also practice real world problems to help you understand how fractions are used every day.

You can find detailed video explanations of each problem in the book by visiting: ArgoPrep.com

WEEK 8 : DAY 1

1. If Roshana ate $\frac{1}{5}$ of the pizza and Reggie ate $\frac{1}{3}$. How much of the pizza remains?

   A. $\frac{6}{8}$ C. $\frac{7}{15}$

   B. $\frac{8}{5}$ D. $\frac{10}{15}$

   5.NF.2

3. How much of a kilometer did Bonnie and Bryson run together?

   A. $\frac{5}{24}$ C. $\frac{2}{10}$

   B. $\frac{5}{12}$ D. $\frac{2}{8}$

   5.NF.1

In a race, 4-person teams each run 1 kilometer. Below you can see how much of a kilometer 3 of the teammates ran. Use the table below to answer questions 2 – 4.

Bryson	$\frac{1}{6}$
Bonnie	$\frac{1}{4}$
Bella	$\frac{1}{3}$

4. What fraction less did Bryson run than Bella?

   A. $\frac{1}{2}$ C. $\frac{1}{4}$

   B. $\frac{1}{3}$ D. $\frac{1}{6}$

   5.NF.1

5. What is 4,098 times 59?

   A. 29,382
   B. 225,392
   C. 241,782
   D. 245,882

2. What fraction of a kilometer did the 4th team member need to run?

   A. $\frac{1}{2}$ C. $\frac{1}{4}$

   B. $\frac{1}{3}$ D. $\frac{1}{6}$

   5.NF.2

   5.NBT.5

TIP of the DAY

Word problems can be fun – imagine you are the one in the story!

WEEK 8 : DAY 2

Mr. Gregory's class took a survey of 5th graders to see what their favorite snack foods were. The results are shown below. Use the results to answer questions 1 – 3.

Granola bars	$\frac{1}{4}$
Peanuts	$\frac{1}{3}$
Raisins	$\frac{1}{12}$
Carrots	$\frac{1}{8}$

1. What fraction of Mr. Gregory's class liked something OTHER than the 4 snacks listed?

   A. $\frac{1}{24}$ C. $\frac{5}{24}$

   B. $\frac{11}{12}$ D. $\frac{7}{12}$

   5.NF.2

2. What fraction of the class liked either granola bars or peanuts?

   A. $\frac{2}{7}$ C. $\frac{5}{24}$

   B. $\frac{11}{12}$ D. $\frac{7}{12}$

   5.NF.1

3. What is the difference between those who liked carrots and those who liked raisins?

   A. $\frac{1}{24}$ C. $\frac{5}{24}$

   B. $\frac{11}{24}$ D. $\frac{7}{24}$

   5.NF.1

4. Bowen thought that $\frac{2}{3} + \frac{1}{4}$ equaled $\frac{3}{7}$. How do you know this answer is incorrect?

   A. 2 + 1 does not equal 3.

   B. $\frac{2}{3} > \frac{3}{7}$ so the answer should be something more than $\frac{2}{3}$.

   C. 3 + 4 does not equal 7.

   D. When adding fractions, you can't have a smaller number in the numerator.

   5.NF.2

TIP of the DAY

When talking about a class, remember that the class is one whole. For example, if $\frac{1}{3}$ of the class was late, then $\frac{2}{3}$ of the class must have been on time.

55

WEEK 8 : DAY 3

Calla and Charles planted grass over the summer. The amount of each type of grass they planted is shown below (in acres). Use this information to answer questions 1 – 4.

Type of Grass	Calla	Charles
Bermuda Grass	$3\frac{1}{8}$	$2\frac{1}{8}$
Kentucky Bluegrass	$4\frac{2}{3}$	$5\frac{7}{9}$
Tall Fescue	$5\frac{1}{4}$	$4\frac{3}{5}$

1. How many acres of Bluegrass were planted by both Calla and Charles?

   A. $10\frac{4}{9}$　　　C. $12\frac{11}{12}$

   B. $11\frac{5}{8}$　　　D. $13\frac{1}{24}$

   5.NF.2

2. How much grass was planted by Calla?

   A. $10\frac{4}{9}$ acres　　　C. $12\frac{11}{12}$ acres

   B. $11\frac{5}{8}$ acres　　　D. $13\frac{1}{24}$ acres

   5.NF.2

3. How many acres of Tall Fescue were planted?

   A. $9\frac{1}{4}$　　　C. $9\frac{3}{4}$

   B. $9\frac{4}{9}$　　　D. $9\frac{17}{20}$

   5.NF.2

4. How much more Tall Fescue was planted than Bermuda?

   A. $4\frac{1}{4}$ acres　　　C. $4\frac{5}{8}$ acres

   B. $4\frac{3}{5}$ acres　　　D. $4\frac{3}{4}$ acres

   5.NF.2

5. What is 3865.6 ÷ 3.2?

   A. 12.08
   B. 120.8
   C. 1208
   D. 12,080

   5.NBT.7

TIP of the DAY

You are learning a lot about fractions and how to add and subtract them – keep up the good work!

56

WEEK 8 : DAY 4

The recreation room was carpeted with 4 different colored carpet squares. Three of the colors and their amounts are shown below. Use the table to answer questions 1 – 3.

Red	$\frac{1}{9}$
Blue	$\frac{2}{3}$
Green	$\frac{1}{6}$

1. What fraction of the carpet squares were yellow?

   A. $\frac{1}{18}$ C. $\frac{7}{18}$

   B. $\frac{5}{18}$ D. $\frac{13}{18}$

   5.NF.2

2. What fraction of the carpet squares were either red or green?

   A. $\frac{1}{18}$ C. $\frac{7}{18}$

   B. $\frac{5}{18}$ D. $\frac{13}{18}$

   5.NF.1

3. What fraction of the carpet squares were either yellow or blue?

   A. $\frac{1}{18}$ C. $\frac{7}{18}$

   B. $\frac{5}{18}$ D. $\frac{13}{18}$

   5.NF.2

4. Which of the following statements is true?

   A. 12.468 < 12.2
   B. 43.16 = 43.160
   C. 118.989 > 119.87
   D. 265.92 < 265.704

   5.NBT.3

5. Look at 542.91. In a different number, the 2 represents a value which is ten times of the value of the 2 in 542.91. What value is represented by the 2 in the other number?

   A. two hundredths
   B. two tenths
   C. two ones
   D. two tens

   5.NBT.1

Be sure to find a common denominator when adding or subtracting fractions or mixed numbers.

WEEK 8 : DAY 5

ASSESSMENT

Four people ate an entire pie. The amount of pie that Christi, Chad and Dallas ate is shown. Dawn's amount is not shown. Use the information to answer questions 1 – 3.

Christi	$\frac{1}{4}$
Chad	$\frac{1}{3}$
Dallas	$\frac{1}{6}$
Dawn	?

1. How much pie did Dawn eat?

   A. $\frac{1}{2}$ C. $\frac{1}{4}$

   B. $\frac{1}{3}$ D. $\frac{1}{12}$

   5.NF.2

2. How much more did Chad eat than Christi?

   A. $\frac{1}{2}$ C. $\frac{1}{4}$

   B. $\frac{1}{3}$ D. $\frac{1}{12}$

   5.NF.1

3. How much did Chad and Dallas eat together?

   A. $\frac{1}{2}$ C. $\frac{1}{4}$

   B. $\frac{1}{3}$ D. $\frac{1}{12}$

   5.NF.1

4. There are two number patterns below.

   Pattern A: 0, 2, 4, 6, 8, …
   Pattern B: 0, 1, 2, 3, 4, …

   Which statement is true about the patterns?

   A. Pattern A has no numbers in common with Pattern B.
   B. Pattern A's sixth number is half of Pattern B's sixth number.
   C. Pattern A's seventh number will be 11.
   D. Pattern A has only even numbers.

   5.OA.3

5. Without actually finding out what $\frac{1}{3} + \frac{2}{5}$ equals, which number below can be ruled out as NOT even a POSSIBLE answer?

   A. $\frac{1}{4}$ C. $\frac{5}{6}$

   B. $\frac{3}{5}$ D. $\frac{7}{8}$

   5.NF.2

DAY 6
Challenge question

Why is it impossible for the equation $\frac{1}{2} + \frac{1}{3} = \frac{1}{4}$ to be true?

5.NF.2

Week 9 allows you practice setting up your own division problems involving fractions using real-world problems. Good luck!

You can find detailed video explanations of each problem in the book by visiting: ArgoPrep.com

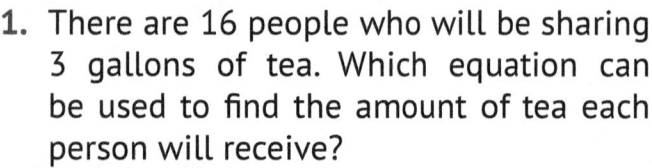

1. There are 16 people who will be sharing 3 gallons of tea. Which equation can be used to find the amount of tea each person will receive?

   A. $16 \times 3 = 48$
   B. $3 \div 16 = \dfrac{3}{16}$
   C. $16 + 3 = 19$
   D. $16 - 3 = 13$

   5.NF.3

2. There will be 10 pounds of flour put evenly into 7 sacks. How many pounds of flour will be in each sack?

   A. $\dfrac{7}{10}$
   B. $\dfrac{10}{7}$
   C. $\dfrac{3}{10}$
   D. $\dfrac{7}{3}$

   5.NF.3

3. If Calista, Chaz and Duane each ate a $\dfrac{2}{3}$ pound burger, how many pounds of hamburger did the restaurant start with?

   A. 0
   B. 1
   C. 2
   D. 3

   5.NF.3

4. What is the value of the expression below?

   $$20 + 8 \div 2 - 6 \times 2$$

   A. 6
   B. 12
   C. 16
   D. 36

   5.OA.1

5. Dustin, Dom and Emma are sharing 4 vanilla and 3 chocolate ice cream sandwiches. Which expression shows how much each person will receive?

   A. $\dfrac{7}{3} = 2\dfrac{2}{3}$
   B. $\dfrac{7}{3} = 2\dfrac{1}{3}$
   C. $\dfrac{3}{7} + \dfrac{4}{7}$
   D. $\dfrac{3}{4} + \dfrac{3}{3}$

   5.NF.3

6. The cheerleaders cut a 44-foot ribbon into 8 equal pieces for hair bows. How much ribbon did each hair bow use?

   A. $5\dfrac{1}{2}$ feet
   B. $5\dfrac{3}{8}$ feet
   C. $5\dfrac{5}{8}$ feet
   D. $5\dfrac{7}{8}$ feet

   5.NF.3

A fraction is really a division problem. $\dfrac{4}{5}$ means that there are 4 "things" being split among 5 people or other items like boxes or days.

60

WEEK 9 : DAY 2

1. A box of noodles is 600 grams and one serving is 45 grams. How many servings are in the box of noodles?

   A. 13
   B. $13\frac{15}{600}$
   C. $13\frac{45}{600}$
   D. $13\frac{15}{45}$

   5.NF.3

2. There are 20 people who will be sharing 56 pounds of coffee beans. How many pounds of coffee beans will each person receive?

   A. $2\frac{1}{5}$
   B. $2\frac{5}{14}$
   C. $2\frac{16}{20}$
   D. $2\frac{16}{56}$

   5.NF.3

3. The workers need to place 123 pounds of apples into crates. If there are 13 crates, how many pounds will be in each crate?

   A. $\frac{13}{123}$
   B. $9\frac{6}{13}$
   C. $9\frac{6}{123}$
   D. $9\frac{13}{123}$

   5.NF.3

4. There were 5000 milliliters of lemonade to be poured into 22 pitchers. How many milliliters of lemonade would each pitcher have?

   A. $227\frac{6}{22}$
   B. $227\frac{6}{5000}$
   C. $227\frac{22}{5000}$
   D. $27\frac{6}{22}$

   5.NF.3

5. Twenty-one homes are being built on 15 acres. How many acres will each home have?

   A. $\frac{15}{21}$
   B. $1\frac{6}{15}$
   C. $1\frac{15}{21}$
   D. $1\frac{6}{21}$

   5.NF.3

6. What is 325.2948 rounded to the nearest hundredth?

   A. 325.295
   B. 325.29
   C. 325.3
   D. 300

   5.NBT.4

TIP of the DAY

In fractions, the denominator (bottom number) indicates the number you are dividing by.

WEEK 9 : DAY 3

Use the chart below to answer questions 1 – 3.

Granola bars	12
Fruit bars	8
Candy bars	20

1. If there are 5 students and all the bars are divided evenly, how many bars will each student get?

   A. 8
   B. $8\frac{1}{5}$
   C. $8\frac{4}{5}$
   D. $8\frac{7}{40}$

   5.NF.3

2. If only the granola bars are divided among the 5 students, how many granola bar will each student get?

   A. $\frac{5}{12}$
   B. $1\frac{2}{5}$
   C. $2\frac{2}{5}$
   D. $2\frac{3}{5}$

   5.NF.3

3. If the fruit and candy bars are divided among the 5 students, how many bars will each student get?

   A. $4\frac{5}{7}$
   B. $5\frac{2}{5}$
   C. $5\frac{3}{5}$
   D. $5\frac{3}{28}$

   5.NF.3

4. If Dinah, Edward and Felix each ate $\frac{4}{3}$ cups of ice cream, how many cups of ice cream were there to start?

   A. 1
   B. 2
   C. 3
   D. 4

   5.NF.3

5. Elijah and Ella each ate $\frac{1}{4}$ of the pizza and Francesca ate $\frac{1}{3}$. How much of the pizza is left?

   A. $\frac{1}{3}$
   B. $\frac{1}{4}$
   C. $\frac{1}{6}$
   D. $\frac{1}{12}$

   5.NF.2

TIP of the DAY

Remember a fraction can be viewed as one number being divided by another number. $\frac{8}{3}$ means that 8 is being divided by 3.

WEEK 9 : DAY 4

1. The trip was 586 miles. If they took 9 days to travel, how many miles did they travel per day?

   A. $65\frac{1}{3}$ C. $65\frac{1}{586}$

   B. $65\frac{1}{9}$ D. $65\frac{9}{586}$

   5.NF.3

2. There are 25 people who will be sharing 11 kg of rice. Which equation can be used to find the amount of rice each person will receive?

   A. $11 \div 25 = \frac{11}{25}$ C. $25 \div 11 = 2\frac{3}{25}$

   B. $25 \div 11 = 2\frac{3}{11}$ D. $25 \div 11 = 2\frac{11}{25}$

   5.NF.3

The chart below shows 3 different trail lengths. Use the information below to answer questions 3 – 4.

Black Bear Trail	25 km
Green River Trail	18 km
Yellow Mountain Trail	19 km

3. If the hikers covered all 3 trails in 4 days, how many km would they need to hike each day?

   A. $15\frac{1}{2}$ C. $15\frac{1}{4}$

   B. $15\frac{1}{3}$ D. $15\frac{1}{5}$

   5.NF.3

4. How many km would they travel per day if they completed the Green River and Yellow Mountain trails in 3 days?

   A. $12\frac{1}{2}$ C. $12\frac{1}{4}$

   B. $12\frac{1}{3}$ D. $12\frac{1}{5}$

   5.NF.3

5. The digit 7 in 86,175 is _____ times the value of the 7 in 13,704.

   A. 10   C. $\frac{1}{10}$

   B. 100   D. $\frac{1}{100}$

   5.NBT.1

TIP of the DAY

Tomorrow when you take the assessment, think through carefully to understand if division is involved and if so, which number is being divided by which number.

WEEK 9 : DAY 5

ASSESSMENT

1. A marathon runner ran 26 miles in 5 hours. About how many miles did she run per hour?

   A. $5\frac{1}{5}$ C. $5\frac{2}{5}$

   B. $5\frac{1}{26}$ D. $5\frac{21}{26}$

   5.NF.3

2. There are 18 people who will each be walking a section of a road that is 168 miles long. If each walker walks the same distance, how many miles will each one walk?

   A. $9\frac{1}{18}$ C. $9\frac{6}{18}$

   B. $9\frac{3}{18}$ D. $9\frac{9}{18}$

   5.NF.3

3. There are 7 cups of yogurt that can be split among 4 people. If everyone gets the same amount, how many cups of yogurt will each person get?

   A. $1\frac{3}{4}$ C. $1\frac{4}{7}$

   B. $1\frac{3}{7}$ D. $1\frac{7}{4}$

   5.NF.3

4. Which statement is true about the values of the two expressions below?

   Expression A: (13 × 261)
   Expression B: 8 × (13 × 261)

   A. The value of Expression A is 8 times the value of Expression B.
   B. The value of Expression B is 8 times the value of Expression A.
   C. The value of Expression A is 8 more than the value of Expression B.
   D. The value of Expression B is 8 more than the value of Expression A.

   5.OA.2

5. The teacher cut a 36-inch roll of paper into 20 equal pieces, one for each student. How much paper did each student receive?

   A. $1\frac{3}{4}$ inches   C. $1\frac{16}{36}$ inches

   B. $1\frac{4}{5}$ inches   D. $1\frac{20}{16}$ inches

   5.NF.3

6. There will be 50 pounds of sugar put evenly into 13 sacks. How many pounds of sugar will be in each sack?

   A. $\frac{13}{27}$ B. $\frac{13}{50}$ C. $\frac{37}{50}$ D. $\frac{50}{13}$

   5.NF.3

DAY 6
Challenge question

There are 11 people on a team. If each team member swims $\frac{9}{11}$ of a mile in the race, how many miles in total was the race?

5.NF.3

WEEK 10

VIDEO EXPLANATIONS

ARGOPREP.COM

CUPCAKES

- flour
- sugar
- baking powder
- butter
- 2 eggs
- milk
- vanilla
- Fine salt

Week 10 lets you try your hand at multiplying fractions by whole numbers and other fractions. You will also calculate areas of different rectangles.

You can find detailed video explanations of each problem in the book by visiting:
ArgoPrep.com

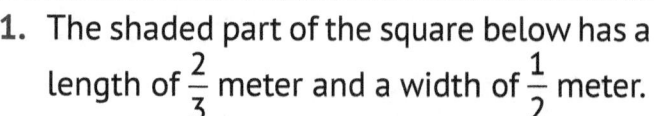

1. The shaded part of the square below has a length of $\frac{2}{3}$ meter and a width of $\frac{1}{2}$ meter.

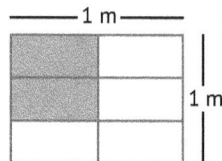

What is the area, in square meters, of the shaded part of the square?

A. $\frac{1}{6}$ B. $\frac{2}{6}$ C. $\frac{3}{6}$ D. $\frac{4}{6}$

5.NF.4

2. Which scenario could be describing the model below?

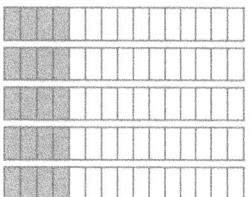

A. On 5 different days, there were $4\frac{15}{100}$ inches of rain.
B. Darius ate $\frac{4}{15}$ of the pizza.
C. Francesca made 4 out of her 15 shots.
D. DJ ran $\frac{4}{15}$ of a mile 5 days last week.

5.NF.4

3. Which mathematical expression is equivalent to the number sentence below?

   Three less than the product of 12 and 13.

   A. 3 − 12 × 13   C. (12 × 13) − 3
   B. 3 − (12 × 13)   D. 12 × (13 − 3)

5.OA.2

4. The dog kennel floor measures $\frac{4}{9}$ meters long and $\frac{3}{5}$ meters wide. What is the area of the kennel floor?

   A. $\frac{7}{14}$ square meters
   B. $\frac{12}{45}$ square meters
   C. $\frac{12}{14}$ square meters
   D. $\frac{7}{45}$ square meters

5.NF.4

5. What is the product of $\frac{3}{5} \times \frac{4}{7}$?

   A. $\frac{12}{35}$ C. $\frac{7}{35}$
   B. $\frac{7}{12}$ D. $\frac{12}{12}$

5.NF.4

TIP of the DAY

When multiplying fractions by whole numbers, remember that a whole number can also be written as a fraction. The number 3 can be written as $\frac{3}{1}$.

WEEK 10 : DAY 2

1. What is the area of the rectangle shown below?

   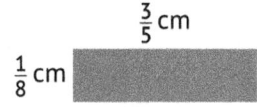

   A. $\dfrac{4}{13}$ cm²   C. $\dfrac{3}{40}$ cm²

   B. $\dfrac{3}{13}$ cm²   D. $\dfrac{4}{40}$ cm²

   5.NF.4

2. What is the product of $\dfrac{3}{4} \times \dfrac{3}{7}$?

   A. $\dfrac{6}{11}$ B. $\dfrac{9}{11}$ C. $\dfrac{6}{28}$ D. $\dfrac{9}{28}$

   5.NF.4

3. The shaded part of the square below has a width of $\dfrac{2}{3}$ yard and a length of $\dfrac{4}{5}$ yard.

   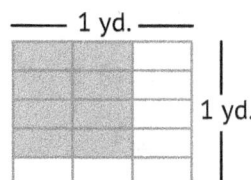

   What is the area, in square yards, of the shaded part of the square?

   A. $\dfrac{6}{8}$ B. $\dfrac{6}{15}$ C. $\dfrac{8}{8}$ D. $\dfrac{8}{15}$

   5.NF.4

4. Which equation is modeled below?

   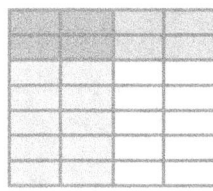

   A. $\dfrac{4}{8} \times \dfrac{4}{10} = \dfrac{16}{80}$

   B. $\dfrac{2}{4} \times \dfrac{2}{7} = \dfrac{4}{28}$

   C. $\dfrac{2}{8} \times \dfrac{4}{14} = \dfrac{8}{112}$

   D. $\dfrac{2}{8} \times \dfrac{2}{14} = \dfrac{4}{112}$

   5.NF.4

5. The rug measures $\dfrac{5}{6}$ foot long and $\dfrac{1}{3}$ foot wide. What is the area of the rug?

   A. $\dfrac{5}{18}$ ft²

   B. $\dfrac{6}{18}$ ft²

   C. $\dfrac{5}{9}$ ft²

   D. $\dfrac{6}{9}$ ft²

   5.NF.4

TIP of the DAY

When multiplying fractions, multiply the numerators together and then multiply the denominators together.

WEEK 10 : DAY 3

1. The shaded part of the square below has a length of $\frac{4}{7}$ foot and a width of $\frac{3}{4}$ foot.

   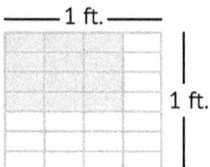

   What is the area, in square feet, of the shaded part of the square?

   A. $\frac{7}{11}$ B. $\frac{7}{28}$ C. $\frac{12}{11}$ D. $\frac{12}{28}$

   5.NF.4

2. Which scenario could describe the model below?

   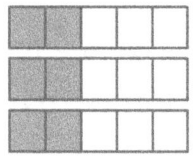

   A. It rained $\frac{2}{5}$ of an inch on 3 different days.
   B. Gela skated $\frac{6}{15}$ of a mile on 3 different days.
   C. Harrison read $\frac{2}{5}$ of the newspaper on 15 different days.
   D. Heidi sliced $\frac{6}{15}$ of the watermelon on 15 different days.

   5.NF.4

3. What is the area of the rectangle shown below?

   $\frac{1}{8}$ in.

   $\frac{3}{8}$ in.

   A. $\frac{3}{16}$ in^2 C. $\frac{4}{16}$ in^2

   B. $\frac{3}{64}$ in^2 D. $\frac{4}{64}$ in^2

   5.NF.4

The table below shows the cost of some books. Use the table to answer questions 4 – 5.

Books	Cost (dollars)
2	8
4	16
6	24

4. What is the cost for 5 books?

   A. $18   B. $20   C. $22   D. $23

   5.OA.3

5. What would you expect the cost of 11 books to be?

   A. $32   B. $35   C. $41   D. $44

   5.OA.3

TIP of the DAY

When a fraction is multiplied by a whole number other than 1, the product is a number between the fraction and the whole number.

WEEK 10 : DAY 4

1. The shaded part of the square below has a length of $\frac{3}{7}$ meter and a width of $\frac{1}{2}$ meter.

   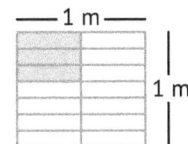

   What is the area, in square meters, of the shaded part of the square?

   A. $\frac{3}{9}$ B. $\frac{3}{14}$ C. $\frac{4}{9}$ D. $\frac{4}{14}$

   5.NF.4

2. Twelve nails have a mass of 423 grams. The number of grams per nail is between what 2 numbers?

   A. 31 and 32   C. 35 and 36
   B. 33 and 34   D. 37 and 38

   5.NF.3

3. What is the area of the rectangle shown below?

   A. $\frac{6}{8}$ cm²   C. $\frac{6}{15}$ cm²
   B. $\frac{8}{9}$ cm²   D. $\frac{8}{15}$ cm²

   5.NF.4

4. What is the product of $\frac{9}{4} \times \frac{3}{11}$?

   A. $\frac{12}{15}$ B. $\frac{27}{15}$ C. $\frac{12}{44}$ D. $\frac{27}{44}$

   5.NF.4

5. The banner measures $\frac{6}{7}$ yards long and $\frac{2}{5}$ yards wide. What is the area of the banner?

   A. $\frac{8}{12}$ yd²   C. $\frac{8}{35}$ yd²
   B. $\frac{12}{13}$ yd²   D. $\frac{12}{35}$ yd²

   5.NF.4

6. Which equation could be modeled below?

   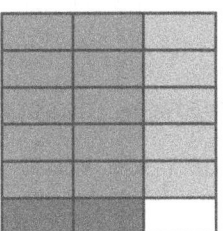

   A. $\frac{2}{3} \times \frac{5}{6} = \frac{10}{18}$ C. $\frac{10}{12} \times \frac{18}{15} = \frac{180}{180}$
   B. $\frac{2}{3} \times \frac{6}{7} = \frac{12}{21}$ D. $\frac{2}{4} \times \frac{5}{6} = \frac{10}{24}$

   5.NF.4

Remember that a factor is a number that is being multiplied. In 5 × 8 = 40, 5 and 8 are the factors and 40 is the product.

WEEK 10 : DAY 5

ASSESSMENT

1. What is the product of $\frac{3}{5} \times \frac{3}{10}$?

   A. $\frac{9}{50}$ C. $\frac{6}{15}$

   B. $\frac{9}{15}$ D. $\frac{6}{50}$

   5.NF.4

2. What is the area of the rectangle shown below?

   $\frac{1}{8}$ mm
   $\frac{7}{12}$ mm

   A. $\frac{7}{20}$ mm²   C. $\frac{7}{96}$ mm²

   B. $\frac{8}{20}$ mm²   D. $\frac{8}{96}$ mm²

   5.NF.4

3. A small blanket measures $\frac{4}{5}$ yards long and $\frac{2}{3}$ yards wide. What is the area of the blanket?

   A. $\frac{6}{8}$ yd²   C. $\frac{8}{15}$ yd²

   B. $\frac{8}{8}$ yd²   D. $\frac{6}{15}$ yd²

   5.NF.4

4. Which scenario could describe the model below?

   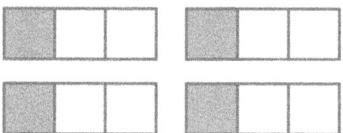

   A. Jessica did homework for $\frac{1}{3}$ of an hour on 12 different days.

   B. James ate $\frac{1}{3}$ of 4 apples.

   C. It rained $\frac{1}{12}$ of an inch on 4 different days.

   D. Heather ate twelve $\frac{1}{3}$-pound burgers.

   5.NF.4

5. There are 80 ounces of turkey that 6 people will share. The number of ounces of turkey each person will get is between what 2 numbers?

   A. 10 and 11
   B. 11 and 12
   C. 12 and 13
   D. 13 and 14

   5.NF.3

DAY 6
Challenge question

A flag measures $\frac{5}{8}$ yard by $\frac{1}{3}$ yard. What is the area of the flag?

5.NF.4

70

WEEK 11

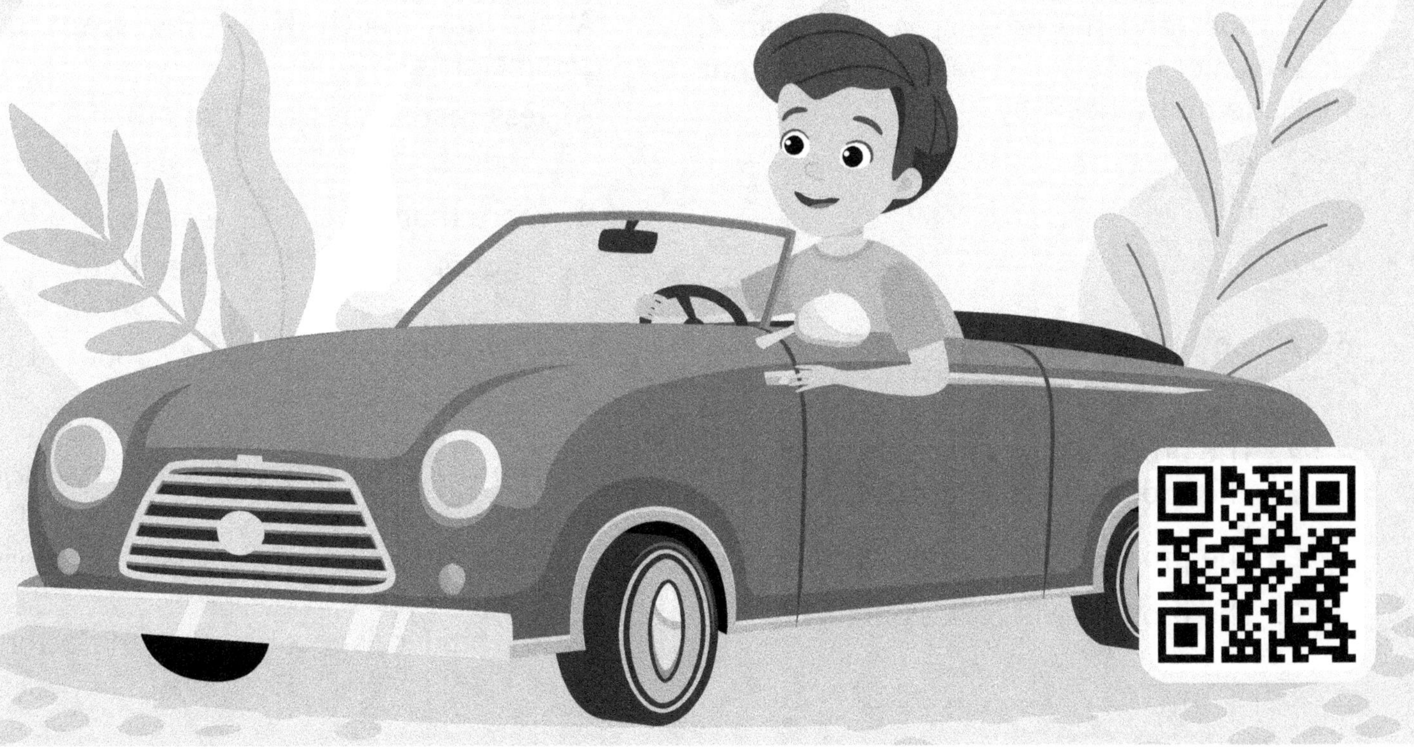

This week (Week 11) you will have a chance to show your understanding of what a product should be, based only on the factors, without even multiplying them out!

You can find detailed video explanations of each problem in the book by visiting: ArgoPrep.com

WEEK 11 : DAY 1

1. Which statement is true about the product of $\frac{3}{5} \times \frac{7}{7}$?
   A. The product is greater than each factor.
   B. The product is less than each factor.
   C. The product is greater than $\frac{3}{5}$ but less than $\frac{47}{7}$.
   D. The product is equal to one of the factors.

   5.NF.5

2. Halle multiplies the number 4 by another number and the product is less than 4. Which of these could be the number that Halle multiplies 4 by?
   A. $\frac{6}{6}$ B. $\frac{6}{5}$ C. $\frac{5}{6}$ D. $\frac{5}{5}$

   5.NF.5

3. Which statement about $\frac{5}{6} \times 12$ is NOT true?
   A. The product will be greater than 1.
   B. The product will be greater than 12.
   C. The product will be greater than $\frac{5}{6}$.
   D. The product will be less than 12.

   5.NF.5

4. Which statement is true about the product of $\frac{3}{5} \times \frac{1}{8}$?
   A. The product is greater than each factor.
   B. The product is less than each factor.
   C. The product is greater than $\frac{1}{8}$ but less than $\frac{3}{5}$.
   D. The product is equal to one of the factors.

   5.NF.5

5. Jeremy watched 7 hours of TV and noticed that $\frac{2}{5}$ of that time were commercials. About how much time was spent on commercials?
   A. less than 7 hours
   B. more than 7 hours
   C. less than $\frac{2}{5}$ of an hour
   D. exactly $\frac{2}{5}$ of an hour

   5.NF.5

6. Which statement is true about the product of $\frac{2}{7} \times 8$?
   A. The product is greater than each factor.
   B. The product is less than each factor.
   C. The product is greater than $\frac{2}{7}$ but less than 8.
   D. The product is equal to one of the factors.

   5.NF.5

TIP of the DAY

If a whole number is multiplied by a fraction that is < 1, the product will be less than that whole number.

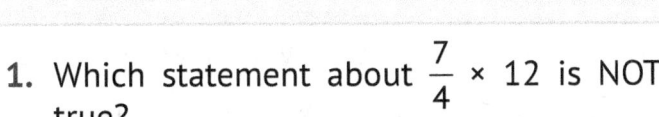

WEEK 11 : DAY 2

1. Which statement about $\frac{7}{4} \times 12$ is NOT true?
   A. The product will be greater than 1.
   B. The product will be greater than 12.
   C. The product will be greater than $\frac{7}{4}$.
   D. The product will be less than 12.

   5.NF.5

2. Josh multiplies the number 6 by another number and the product is more than 6. Which of these could be the number that Josh multiplies 6 by?
   A. $\frac{6}{6}$ B. $\frac{6}{5}$ C. $\frac{5}{6}$ D. $\frac{5}{5}$

   5.NF.5

3. Which statement is true about the product of $\frac{8}{6} \times \frac{9}{8}$?
   A. The product is greater than each factor.
   B. The product is less than each factor.
   C. The product is greater than $\frac{9}{8}$ but less than $\frac{8}{5}$.
   D. The product is equal to one of the factors.

   5.NF.5

4. Johanna fished for 12 hours. Her brother fished with her for $\frac{2}{3}$ of that time. How much time did Johanna spend with her brother fishing?
   A. more than 12 hours
   B. less than 12 hours
   C. less than $\frac{2}{3}$ of an hour
   D. exactly $\frac{2}{3}$ of an hour

   5.NF.5

5. Which statement is true about the product of $\frac{1}{4} \times \frac{3}{8}$?
   A. The product is greater than each factor.
   B. The product is less than each factor.
   C. The product is greater than $\frac{1}{4}$ but less than $\frac{3}{8}$.
   D. The product is equal to one of the factors.

   5.NF.5

6. Eighteen tons of concrete were split among 12 job sites. How many tons of concrete will be used at each site?
   A. $\frac{12}{18}$ B. $1\frac{1}{2}$ C. $1\frac{2}{3}$ D. $1\frac{6}{18}$

   5.NF.3

TIP of the DAY

If a whole number is multiplied by an improper fraction > 1, the product will be more than that whole number.

73

WEEK 11 : DAY 3

1. Which statement about $8 \times \frac{9}{9}$ is true?

   A. The product will be greater than 8.
   B. The product will be less than 1.
   C. The product will be greater than $\frac{9}{9}$.
   D. The product will be less than 8.

   5.NF.5

2. Kiera multiplies the number 3 by another number and the product is less than 3. Which of these could be the number that Kiera multiplies 3 by?

   A. $\frac{8}{11}$ C. $\frac{5}{5}$
   B. $\frac{9}{3}$ D. $\frac{4}{3}$

   5.NF.5

3. Which statement is true about the product of $11 \times \frac{4}{9}$?

   A. The product is greater than $\frac{4}{9}$ but less than 11.
   B. The product is greater than each factor.
   C. The product is less than each factor.
   D. The product is equal to one of the factors.

   5.NF.5

4. Iris is saving to buy a new computer. Each month she saves up $\frac{2}{9}$ of the cost of the computer. After 9 months which statement would be true?

   A. Iris still does not have enough money for a computer.
   B. Iris has saved enough money for 2 computers.
   C. Iris has exactly enough money for 1 computer.
   D. Iris has saved exactly enough money for 3 computers.

   5.NF.5

5. What is the product of 2,860 and 412?

   A. 995,720   C. 1,087,230
   B. 997,730   D. 1,178,320

   5.NBT.5

6. Which statement is true about the product of $19 \times \frac{3}{7}$?

   A. The product is greater than each factor.
   B. The product is less than each factor.
   C. The product is greater than $\frac{3}{7}$ but less than 19.
   D. The product is equal to one of the factors.

   5.NF.5

TIP of the DAY

If a fraction is multiplied by a number that is equal to the number 1, then the product will be equal to the original fraction.

WEEK 11 : DAY 4

1. If Julia mows $\frac{1}{4}$ of an acre per hour, which statement would be true after 7 hours?
   A. Julia mowed exactly 2 acres.
   B. Julia would not have mowed a complete acre.
   C. Julia mowed more than 1 acre.
   D. Julia mowed exactly 1 acre.

   5.NF.5

2. Gemma rode her bike for 8 hours. She picked some flowers and had to ride with them in her hand for $\frac{1}{4}$ of the time. How much time was Gemma riding while holding the flowers?
   A. less than 8 hours
   B. more than 8 hours
   C. less than $\frac{1}{4}$ of an hour
   D. exactly $\frac{1}{4}$ of an hour

   5.NF.5

3. Which statement is true about the product of $\frac{3}{8} \times 23$?
   A. The product is greater than each factor.
   B. The product is less than each factor.
   C. The product is greater than $\frac{3}{8}$ but less than 23.
   D. The product is equal to one of the factors.

   5.NF.5

4. Evan had to pack 5,275 pairs of socks into boxes that could hold 25 pairs each. How many boxes would Evan need to pack all of the socks?
   A. 201   C. 221
   B. 211   D. 241

   5.NBT.6

5. Jonah multiplies the number 11 by another number and the product is 11. Which of these could be the number that Jonah multiplies 11 by?
   A. $\frac{8}{11}$ C. $\frac{7}{7}$
   B. $\frac{11}{5}$ D. $\frac{5}{3}$

   5.NF.5

6. Which statement is true about the product of $\frac{3}{3} \times \frac{6}{7}$?
   A. The product is greater than each factor.
   B. The product is less than each factor.
   C. The product is greater than $\frac{6}{7}$ but less than $\frac{3}{3}$.
   D. The product is equal to one of the factors.

   5.NF.5

TIP of the DAY

When multiplying by a fraction, try to find out if the fraction is < 1, > 1 or = 1. This step will help you check your answer.

WEEK 11 : DAY 5

ASSESSMENT

1. If Lydia crochets $\frac{2}{7}$ of a blanket per hour, which statement would be true after 5 hours?
   A. Lydia crocheted more than 1 blanket.
   B. Lydia would not have completed 1 blanket.
   C. Lydia would have crocheted exactly 2 blankets.
   D. Lydia would have crocheted exactly 1 blanket.

   5.NF.5

2. Eva multiplies the number 8 by another number and the product is < 8. Which of these could be the number that Eva multiplies 8 by?
   A. $\frac{8}{11}$ B. $\frac{11}{5}$ C. $\frac{7}{7}$ D. $\frac{5}{3}$

   5.NF.5

3. Which statement is true about the product of $\frac{7}{4} \times \frac{5}{3}$?
   A. The product is greater than each factor.
   B. The product is less than each factor.
   C. The product is greater than $\frac{7}{4}$ but less than $\frac{5}{3}$.
   D. The product is equal to one of the factors.

   5.NF.5

4. Martin drove $\frac{1}{9}$ of the trip in 1 hour. Which statement would be true if Martin drove for 8 hours?
   A. Martin would have completed the trip before 8 hours.
   B. Martin would not have completed the trip.
   C. Martin would have completed the trip and been able to start back.
   D. Martin would have completed the trip after exactly 8 hours.

   5.NF.5

5. Which statement about $\frac{4}{3} \times 9$ is NOT true?
   A. The product will be greater than 1.
   B. The product will be greater than 9.
   C. The product will be greater than $\frac{4}{3}$.
   D. The product will be less than 9.

   5.NF.5

DAY 6
Challenge question

Write a statement that says what you would expect the product to be for $\frac{7}{8} \times 7$.

5.NF.5

Often students really struggle with understanding fractions, so Week 12 will give you lots of extra practice with real-world problems that involve fractions.

You can find detailed video explanations of each problem in the book by visiting: ArgoPrep.com

WEEK 12 : DAY 1

1. Lexie ran for $4\frac{1}{5}$ hours last week. Malia ran $2\frac{1}{2}$ as long. Which equation could be used to find out how many hours Malia ran last week?

    A. $4\frac{1}{5} \times 2\frac{1}{2} = 10\frac{1}{10}$ C. $4\frac{1}{5} \times 2\frac{1}{2} = 6\frac{1}{10}$

    B. $4\frac{1}{5} \times 2\frac{1}{2} = 10\frac{1}{2}$ D. $4\frac{1}{5} \times 2\frac{1}{2} = 8\frac{1}{10}$

    5.NF.6

2. What is the product of $\frac{8}{5} \times \frac{9}{7}$?

    A. $\frac{17}{35}$ B. $1\frac{5}{12}$ C. $2\frac{2}{35}$ D. 6

    5.NF.4

Below is a chart showing how many hours some students spent studying over the weekend. Use the information to answer questions 3 – 5.

Katherine	$6\frac{2}{5}$
Jerome	$5\frac{1}{5}$
Lena	$4\frac{3}{8}$

3. If Layla studied half as much as Jerome, how long did Layla study?

    A. $2\frac{3}{5}$ hours   C. $6\frac{1}{4}$ hours

    B. $4\frac{4}{5}$ hours   D. $8\frac{3}{4}$ hours

    5.NF.6

4. If Jose studied twice as long as Lena, how long did Jose study?

    A. $2\frac{3}{5}$ hours   C. $6\frac{1}{4}$ hours

    B. $4\frac{4}{5}$ hours   D. $8\frac{3}{4}$ hours

    5.NF.6

5. If Kelvin studied $\frac{3}{4}$ as long as Katherine, how long did Kelvin study?

    A. $2\frac{3}{5}$ hours   C. $6\frac{1}{4}$ hours

    B. $4\frac{4}{5}$ hours   D. $8\frac{3}{4}$ hours

    5.NF.6

TIP of the DAY

When multiplying a mixed number, remember to change it to an improper fraction first.

78

WEEK 12 : DAY 2

Below is a chart showing how many cups of coffee some teachers drank last week. Use the information to answer questions 1 – 3.

Ms. Abbas	$6\frac{1}{4}$
Mr. Lenox	$10\frac{1}{2}$
Mrs. Shirlen	$8\frac{2}{5}$

1. If Mrs. Canipe drank $\frac{2}{3}$ as much coffee as Mr. Lenox, how much coffee did Mrs. Canipe drink?

   A. 5 cups C. 12 cups
   B. 7 cups D. 21 cups

   5.NF.6

2. If Miss Mason drank $\frac{4}{5}$ as much coffee as Ms. Abbas, how much coffee did Miss Mason drink?

   A. 5 cups C. 12 cups
   B. 7 cups D. 21 cups

   5.NF.6

3. If Mr. McSwain drank $2\frac{1}{2}$ times as much coffee as Mrs. Shirlen, how much coffee did Mr. McSwain drink?

   A. 5 cups C. 12 cups
   B. 7 cups D. 21 cups

   5.NF.6

4. Over the summer Janelle grew $2\frac{1}{4}$ inches and Keith grew $1\frac{4}{5}$ inches. How many inches did they grow combined?

   A. $3\frac{1}{2}$ C. $4\frac{1}{20}$
   B. $3\frac{5}{9}$ D. $4\frac{5}{20}$

   5.NF.1

5. Jacoby bought $7\frac{1}{2}$ gallons of milk. Gwen bought half that amount of milk. Which equation could be used to find out how many gallons of milk Gwen bought?

   A. $7\frac{1}{2} \times 2 = 15$ C. $7\frac{1}{2} \times \frac{1}{2} = 7\frac{2}{4}$
   B. $7\frac{1}{2} \times 2 = 14\frac{1}{2}$ D. $7\frac{1}{2} \times \frac{1}{2} = 3\frac{3}{4}$

   5.NF.6

TIP of the DAY

After finding the product of fractions or mixed numbers, be sure to check your answer to make sure it is a reduced answer.

WEEK 12 : DAY 3

1. Mike worked for $3\frac{4}{4}$ hours on Saturday. On Sunday he worked $\frac{1}{3}$ as long. Which equation could be used to find out how many hours Mike worked on Sunday?

   A. $3\frac{3}{4} \times 3 = 9\frac{3}{4}$
   C. $3\frac{3}{4} \times \frac{1}{3} = 1\frac{3}{4}$
   B. $3\frac{3}{4} \times 3 = 11\frac{1}{4}$
   D. $3\frac{3}{4} \times \frac{1}{3} = 1\frac{1}{4}$

   5.NF.6

See how many pans of brownies Joel ate below. Use the drawing to answer questions 2 – 4.

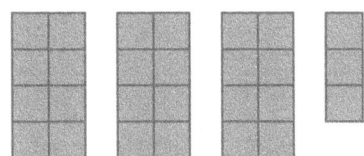

2. If Lana ate $\frac{1}{3}$ as many brownies as Joel, how many pans of brownies did Lana eat?

   A. $1\frac{1}{8}$
   C. $6\frac{3}{4}$
   B. $3\frac{1}{2}$
   D. 9

   5.NF.6

3. Gavin ate $2\frac{2}{3}$ times as many brownies as Joel. How many pans of brownies did Gavin eat?

   A. $1\frac{1}{8}$
   C. $6\frac{3}{4}$
   B. $3\frac{1}{2}$
   D. 9

   5.NF.6

4. Ian ate double what Joel ate. How many pans of brownies did Ian eat?

   A. $1\frac{1}{8}$
   C. $6\frac{3}{4}$
   B. $3\frac{1}{2}$
   D. 9

   5.NF.6

5. What is the area of the rectangle below?

   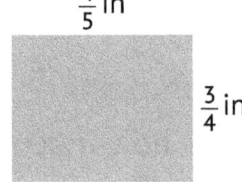

   A. $\frac{3}{5}$ in^2
   C. $\frac{7}{9}$ in^2
   B. $\frac{4}{6}$ in^2
   D. $\frac{7}{20}$ in^2

   5.NF.4

TIP of the DAY

You are doing a fabulous job working through the fraction sections – keep it up!

WEEK 12 : DAY 4

1. Larissa owns $8\frac{3}{5}$ acres of land. Matt owns 3 times that amount of land. Which equation could be used to find out how many acres Matt owns?

   A. $8\frac{3}{5} \times 3 = 25\frac{4}{5}$ C. $8\frac{3}{5} \times 3 = 24\frac{3}{5}$

   B. $8\frac{3}{5} \times \frac{1}{3} = 5\frac{3}{15}$ D. $8\frac{3}{5} \times \frac{1}{3} = 8\frac{3}{15}$

   5.NF.6

2. One batch of cookies calls for $\frac{3}{4}$ cups of chocolate chips. If Lisa makes $3\frac{1}{2}$ batches of cookies, how many cups of chocolate chips will she need?

   A. $2\frac{5}{8}$ B. $2\frac{3}{4}$ C. $3\frac{3}{8}$ D. $4\frac{1}{4}$

   5.NF.6

3. Katie and Grant picked $25\frac{3}{5}$ bushels of blueberries this year. Next year they hope to pick $1\frac{1}{2}$ times that amount. How many bushels are they hoping to pick next year?

   A. $26\frac{4}{5}$ B. $28\frac{3}{5}$ C. $33\frac{1}{5}$ D. $38\frac{2}{5}$

   5.NF.6

4. Which statement is true about the product of $\frac{4}{4} \times \frac{5}{6}$?

   A. The product is greater than each factor.
   B. The product is less than each factor.
   C. The product is greater than $\frac{5}{6}$ but less than $\frac{4}{4}$.
   D. The product is equal to one of the factors.

   5.NF.5

5. Francis was able to cut up 12 watermelons. If Misty cut up $2\frac{1}{5}$ times as many melons, how many watermelons did Misty cut?

   A. $27\frac{3}{5}$ B. $26\frac{2}{5}$ C. $24\frac{1}{5}$ D. $14\frac{1}{5}$

   5.NF.6

6. Which mathematical expression is equivalent to the number sentence below?

   Sixteen times the sum of 8 and 14.

   A. 8 + 14 × 16
   B. (8 + 14) × 16
   C. 16 × 8 + 14
   D. 16 × (14 − 8)

   5.OA.2

TIP of the DAY

Tomorrow take your time to really understand each question and then check each answer to see if it makes sense.

WEEK 12 : DAY 5

ASSESSMENT

1. One serving of tea has 2 teaspoons of tea leaves. If a pot contains $8\frac{2}{3}$ servings, how many teaspoons of tea leaves are needed for a pot of tea?

   A. $10\frac{2}{3}$ B. $16\frac{2}{3}$ C. $17\frac{1}{3}$ D. $18\frac{1}{3}$

   5.NF.6

2. Which statement is true about the product of $\frac{5}{7} \times \frac{9}{8}$?

   A. The product is greater than each factor.
   B. The product is less than each factor.
   C. The product is greater than $\frac{5}{7}$ but less than $\frac{9}{8}$.
   D. The product is equal to one of the factors.

   5.NF.5

3. Movie A was $3\frac{3}{4}$ hours long. Movie B was only $\frac{2}{3}$ as long. How many hours long was Movie B?

   A. $2\frac{1}{2}$ B. $2\frac{1}{4}$ C. $2\frac{7}{12}$ D. $2\frac{2}{3}$

   5.NF.6

4. Two years ago Junior grew $3\frac{1}{3}$ inches. This year he only grew half that amount. How many inches did Junior grow this year?

   A. $1\frac{1}{6}$ B. $1\frac{1}{2}$ C. $1\frac{2}{3}$ D. $1\frac{3}{4}$

   5.NF.6

5. Which statement is true about the product of $\frac{2}{5} \times \frac{1}{3}$?

   A. The product is greater than each factor.
   B. The product is less than each factor.
   C. The product is greater than $\frac{1}{3}$ but less than $\frac{2}{5}$.
   D. The product is equal to one of the factors.

   5.NF.5

6. Michelle practiced her oboe for $2\frac{1}{3}$ hours. Monica practiced 4 times that long. Which equation could be used to find how long Monica practiced?

   A. $2\frac{1}{3} \times 4 = 8\frac{1}{3}$ C. $2\frac{1}{3} \times \frac{1}{4} = 2\frac{1}{12}$
   B. $2\frac{1}{3} \times 4 = 9\frac{1}{3}$ D. $2\frac{1}{3} \times \frac{1}{4} = 2\frac{2}{7}$

   5.NF.6

DAY 6 Challenge question

Mya spent $2\frac{1}{3}$ hours working on her paper. Nichole spent 3 times that and Nate spent half as much time on their papers. How many hours did Nichole and Nate spend on their papers?

5.NF.6

WEEK 13

Unit fractions are fractions that have a 1 in the numerator. Week 13 will offer lots of exercises that involve the multiplication or division of unit fractions.

You can find detailed video explanations of each problem in the book by visiting: ArgoPrep.com

WEEK 13 : DAY 1

1. What is the value of the expression: $\frac{1}{5} \div 8$?

   A. $\frac{1}{3}$
   B. $\frac{1}{40}$
   C. 3
   D. 40

   5.NF.7

2. There was $\frac{1}{8}$ of a gallon of juice left. If 3 children shared it, how many gallons would each child have?

   A. $\frac{1}{24}$
   B. 24
   C. $\frac{1}{11}$
   D. 11

   5.NF.7

3. What is the value of the expression: $12 \div \frac{1}{4}$?

   A. $\frac{1}{3}$
   B. $\frac{1}{48}$
   C. 3
   D. 48

   5.NF.7

4. Lucy, Jimmy and Karla equally shared $\frac{1}{2}$ of a pizza. Which fraction of the whole pizza did they each receive?

   A. $\frac{2}{3}$
   B. $\frac{1}{6}$
   C. $\frac{1}{3}$
   D. $\frac{1}{2}$

   5.NF.7

5. Cecelia had 4 dollars her mom gave her for fair tickets. If each ticket costs $\frac{1}{2}$ of a dollar, how many tickets could Cecelia purchase?

   A. 1   B. 2   C. 4   D. 8

   5.NF.7

6. Which statement is true about the product of $\frac{2}{2} \times 5$?

   A. The product is greater than each factor.
   B. The product is less than each factor.
   C. The product is greater than $\frac{2}{2}$ but less than 5.
   D. The product is equal to one of the factors.

   5.NF.5

TIP of the DAY

Remember, to divide by a fraction, you multiply by its reciprocal.

WEEK 13 : DAY 2

1. How many $\frac{1}{3}$-cup servings are in 12 cups of coffee?

   A. 4
   B. 12
   C. 36
   D. 48

   5.NF.7

2. What is the value of the expression: $21 \div \frac{1}{3}$?

   A. 63
   B. 7
   C. $\frac{1}{7}$
   D. $\frac{1}{63}$

   5.NF.7

3. Karen and her 2 sisters split a $\frac{1}{2}$ gallon of ice cream. How much ice cream did each girl receive?

   A. $\frac{1}{6}$ gallon
   B. $\frac{1}{4}$ gallon
   C. $\frac{1}{3}$ gallon
   D. $\frac{1}{2}$ gallon

   5.NF.7

4. What is the area of the rectangle below?

   $\frac{2}{5}$ m by $\frac{4}{5}$ m

   A. $\frac{3}{5}$ square meters
   B. $\frac{6}{25}$ square meters
   C. $\frac{8}{25}$ square meters
   D. $1\frac{3}{5}$ square meters

   5.NF.4

5. What is the value of the expression: $16 \div \frac{1}{3}$?

   A. $\frac{3}{16}$
   B. $5\frac{1}{3}$
   C. $\frac{1}{48}$
   D. 48

   5.NF.7

6. Which of the following number sentences is true?

   A. 3.98 > 4
   B. 16.19 = 16.019
   C. 341.4 < 341.387
   D. 47.5 > 47.408

   5.NBT.3

TIP of the DAY

When dividing with fractions and whole numbers, be sure to put the dividend and the divisor in the correct order.

WEEK 13 : DAY 3

At the end of camp, there were some drinks leftover. They are shown below. Use the information to answer questions 1 – 4.

Soda pop	$\frac{1}{4}$ gallon
Tea	$\frac{1}{2}$ gallon
Fruit punch	$\frac{1}{3}$ gallon

1. If 2 people split the soda pop, how many gallons would each person have?

   A. $\frac{1}{6}$ C. 6

   B. $\frac{1}{8}$ D. 8

   5.NF.7

2. If 3 people split the fruit punch, how many gallons would each person receive?

   A. $\frac{1}{9}$ C. 9

   B. $\frac{1}{3}$ D. 3

   5.NF.7

3. The tea was shared by 5 people. How many gallons did each person receive?

   A. 10   C. $\frac{1}{3}$

   B. 3   D. $\frac{1}{10}$

   5.NF.7

4. If there was $2\frac{3}{5}$ times as much lemonade as soda pop, how many gallons of lemonade were there?

   A. $\frac{13}{20}$ C. $2\frac{17}{20}$

   B. $1\frac{7}{13}$ D. $2\frac{4}{7}$

   5.NF.6

5. What is the product of 35.08 and 10^4?

   A. 35.080000
   B. 3508
   C. 35080
   D. 350,800

   5.NBT.2

TIP of the DAY

A reciprocal is a number where the digits change from numerator to denominator and denominator to numerator. The reciprocal of $\frac{1}{4}$ is $\frac{4}{1}$.

86

WEEK 13 : DAY 4

1. What is the value of the expression: $6 \div \frac{1}{5}$?

   A. 30
   B. $\frac{5}{6}$
   C. $1\frac{1}{5}$
   D. $\frac{1}{30}$

   5.NF.7

2. If Eric, Murray and Devin walk a combined total of $\frac{1}{6}$ of a mile, how many miles does each one walk?

   A. $\frac{1}{2}$
   B. $\frac{1}{3}$
   C. $\frac{1}{9}$
   D. $\frac{1}{18}$

   5.NF.7

3. Which number below *could* round to 7,500?

   A. 7,360
   B. 7,451
   C. 7,578
   D. 7,601

   5.NBT.4

4. How many $\frac{1}{4}$-cup servings are in 10 cups of pudding?

   A. 40
   B. 20
   C. $2\frac{1}{2}$
   D. 2

   5.NF.7

5. What is the value of the expression: $\frac{1}{3} \div 5$?

   A. 15
   B. $\frac{1}{15}$
   C. $1\frac{2}{3}$
   D. $\frac{3}{5}$

   5.NF.7

6. Which number has a 6 that is $\frac{1}{10}$ the value of the 6 in 16,480?

   A. 17,936
   B. 29,564
   C. 365,412
   D. 71,640

   5.NBT.1

TIP of the DAY

If a pound is divided into thirds, each of the 3 pieces is $\frac{1}{3}$ of the pound.

WEEK 13 : DAY 5

ASSESSMENT

1. Jax and Kris share $\frac{1}{3}$ of a box of cookies. What fraction of the box does each boy eat?

   A. $\frac{1}{2}$ C. $\frac{1}{5}$

   B. $\frac{1}{3}$ D. $\frac{1}{6}$

   5.NF.7

2. How many $\frac{1}{4}$ gallons are in 6 gallons of gas?

   A. 48
   B. 24
   C. 12
   D. $2\frac{1}{2}$

   5.NF.7

3. What is the value of the expression: $4 \div \frac{1}{4}$?

   A. 1
   B. 4
   C. 16
   D. $\frac{1}{16}$

   5.NF.7

4. Noah multiplies the number 3 by another number and the product is > 3. Which of these could be the number that Noah multiplies 3 by?

   A. $\frac{9}{10}$ B. $\frac{5}{5}$ C. $\frac{7}{3}$ D. $\frac{1}{8}$

   5.NF.5

5. Omar has $\frac{1}{2}$ of a bag of almonds to share with his 4 siblings. What fraction of a bag does each of the 5 siblings receive?

   A. $\frac{1}{6}$ B. $\frac{1}{7}$ C. $\frac{1}{8}$ D. $\frac{1}{10}$

   5.NF.7

6. Which statement is true about the product of $\frac{5}{5} \times \frac{4}{3}$?

   A. The product is greater than each factor.
   B. The product is less than each factor.
   C. The product is greater than $\frac{5}{5}$ but less than $\frac{4}{3}$.
   D. The product is equal to one of the factors.

   5.NF.5

DAY 6
Challenge question

There is $\frac{7}{8}$ of a box of raisins that will be shared by 5 people. What fraction of the box will each person receive?

5.NF.7

WEEK 14

VIDEO EXPLANATIONS — ARGOPREP.COM

This week (Week 14) will require a lot of converting units. Converting units is just another way to say changing units. You will be asked to change yards to inches or kilograms to grams and to make other unit conversions.

You can find detailed video explanations of each problem in the book by visiting: ArgoPrep.com

WEEK 14 : DAY 1

1. The statue weighed 6 pounds and 3 ounces. How many ounces did the statue weigh?

   A. 63
   B. 75
   C. 90
   D. 99

   5.MD.1

2. Noelle is 4 feet tall and her brother Oliver is 42 inches. How many inches taller is Noelle than Oliver?

   A. 4
   B. 6
   C. 18
   D. 38

   5.MD.1

3. Olivia ran 4 km and Peter ran 5,186 m. How much farther did Peter run?

   A. 1,186 meters
   B. 1,186 kilometers
   C. 5,182 meters
   D. 5,182 kilometers

   5.MD.1

4. Annabelle needs 7 kilometers of yarn. Each package has 2,500 meters. How many packages does Annabelle need?

   A. 1
   B. 2
   C. 3
   D. 4

   5.MD.1

5. The "rule" is subtract 3. What is the next number after 28?

   A. 31
   B. 27
   C. 25
   D. 24

   5.OA.3

TIP of the DAY

When comparing length or mass, be sure that you are not only comparing the numbers but also their units.

WEEK 14 : DAY 2

Philip measured 4 snakes he worked with at the zoo and their lengths are shown below. Use this information to answer questions 1 – 3.

Snake A	2 feet
Snake B	38 inches
Snake C	2 yards
Snake D	45 inches

1. Which statement below is true?

   A. Snake B is longer than Snake D.
   B. Snake B is longer than Snake A.
   C. Snake A is longer than Snake C.
   D. Snake C is longer than Snakes B and D combined.

   5.MD.1

2. Which snake is the shortest?

   A. A
   B. B
   C. C
   D. D

   5.MD.1

3. Which snakes are the 2 longest?

   A. Snakes A and B
   B. Snakes B and C
   C. Snakes A and D
   D. Snakes C and D

   5.MD.1

4. The bag of potatoes weighs 8 pounds and 2 ounces. The sack of onions weighs 6 pounds 12 ounces. How much heavier are the potatoes?

   A. 1 pound, 6 ounces
   B. 1 pound, 10 ounces
   C. 2 pounds, 4 ounces
   D. 2 pound, 10 ounces

   5.MD.1

5. Five people each drank $\frac{4}{5}$ cup of coffee. How many cups of coffee did they share?

   A. 2
   B. 3
   C. 4
   D. 5

   5.NF.3

TIP of the DAY

The Metric System is based upon the number 10, which makes it easier to convert between metric units.

WEEK 14 : DAY 3

1. The building is 421 meters tall. How tall is the building in centimeters?

   A. 4.21
   B. 4,210
   C. 42,100
   D. 421,000

   5.MD.1

2. The football player ran for 53 yards. How many inches did he run?

   A. 159
   B. 1,760
   C. 1,908
   D. 2,862

   5.MD.1

3. Les had 8 hours to take his pre-med test. If the test had 185 questions and he spent $2\frac{1}{2}$ minutes on each question, how much time would he have left after completing the test?

   A. $17\frac{1}{2}$ minutes
   B. $\frac{1}{2}$ hour
   C. $1\frac{5}{6}$ hours
   D. 295 minutes

   5.MD.1

4. The race was 15 miles long. How many yards was the race?

   A. 26,400
   B. 79,200
   C. 237,800
   D. 316,800

   5.MD.1

5. Paul was putting stone onto a $25\frac{1}{3}$-yard walkway. He only has 11 feet left to finish. How many yards have been completed?

   A. $14\frac{1}{3}$
   B. $20\frac{1}{3}$
   C. $21\frac{2}{3}$
   D. 29

   5.MD.1

6. What is the value of $\frac{3}{4} + \frac{4}{5}$?

   A. $3\frac{4}{9}$
   B. $1\frac{11}{20}$
   C. $\frac{7}{20}$
   D. $\frac{7}{9}$

   5.NF.1

TIP of the DAY

When changing non-metric units, make sure to use the correct numbers, as they are all different (i.e. 12 in = 1 ft, 60 min = 1 hr, 5,280 ft = 1 mile).

WEEK 14 : DAY 4

The chart below shows the weights of 4 different farm animals. Use the chart to answer questions 1 – 3.

Chicken	$5\frac{1}{5}$ pounds
Pig	$25\frac{3}{4}$ pounds
Goat	305 ounces
Dog	245 ounces

1. Which animal weighs the most?

   A. Chicken
   B. Pig
   C. Goat
   D. Dog

   5.MD.1

2. Which statement is true about the weights of the farm animals?

   A. Pig < Dog
   B. Chicken > Goat
   C. Dog > Chicken
   D. Goat > Pig

   5.MD.1

3. What is the difference in the weights of the goat and dog, in pounds?

   A. $2\frac{3}{4}$ C. $3\frac{3}{4}$
   B. $2\frac{4}{5}$ D. $3\frac{5}{16}$

   5.MD.1

4. The stamp is 71 millimeters wide. How many meters wide is the stamp?

   A. 0.071
   B. 710
   C. 7,100
   D. 71,000

   5.MD.1

5. Which statement is true about the product of $\frac{3}{2} \times \frac{7}{5}$?

   A. The product is greater than both factors.
   B. The product is less than either factor.
   C. The product is greater than $\frac{3}{2}$ but less than $\frac{7}{5}$.
   D. The product is equal to one of the factors.

   5.NF.5

Before tomorrow's assessment, review the numbers you will need to change units between feet/yards, seconds/hours, pounds/ounces, etc.

93

WEEK 14 : DAY 5

ASSESSMENT

1. One bag contained 3 kilograms of sugar. Each cup of coffee had 14 grams of sugar. If there were 200 cups of coffee, how much sugar remained in the bag?

   A. 0.002 kg
   B. 0.02 kg
   C. 0.2 kg
   D. 2 kg

   5.MD.1

2. The bag of oranges weighs 3 pounds and 12 ounces. The bag of apples weighs 6 pounds 4 ounces. How much heavier are the apples?

   A. $2\frac{1}{2}$ pounds   C. $3\frac{1}{2}$ pounds

   B. $2\frac{2}{3}$ pounds   D. $3\frac{2}{3}$ pounds

   5.MD.1

3. What is $\frac{3}{5} \times \frac{1}{3}$?

   A. $\frac{1}{5}$ C. $\frac{3}{8}$

   B. $\frac{1}{2}$ D. $\frac{4}{15}$

   5.NF.4

The weights of 4 turtles were recorded and shown below. Use the table to answer questions 4 – 5.

Turtle A	12 ounces
Turtle B	$1\frac{1}{8}$ pounds
Turtle C	$\frac{3}{4}$ pound
Turtle D	21 ounces

4. Which 2 turtles weighed the same amount?

   A. A and B
   B. C and D
   C. A and C
   D. B and D

   5.MD.1

5. Which turtle weighed the most?

   A. A
   B. B
   C. C
   D. D

   5.MD.1

DAY 6
Challenge question

Each foot of material costs $2.49. Kacie is making 2 patterns. One calls for 3 yards and the other calls for 8 feet of material. How much would it cost to buy the material needed?

5.MD.1, 5.NBT.7

WEEK 15

ARGOPREP.COM

VIDEO EXPLANATIONS

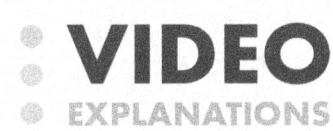

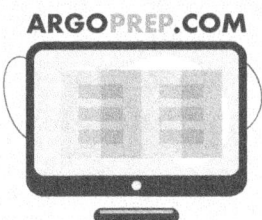

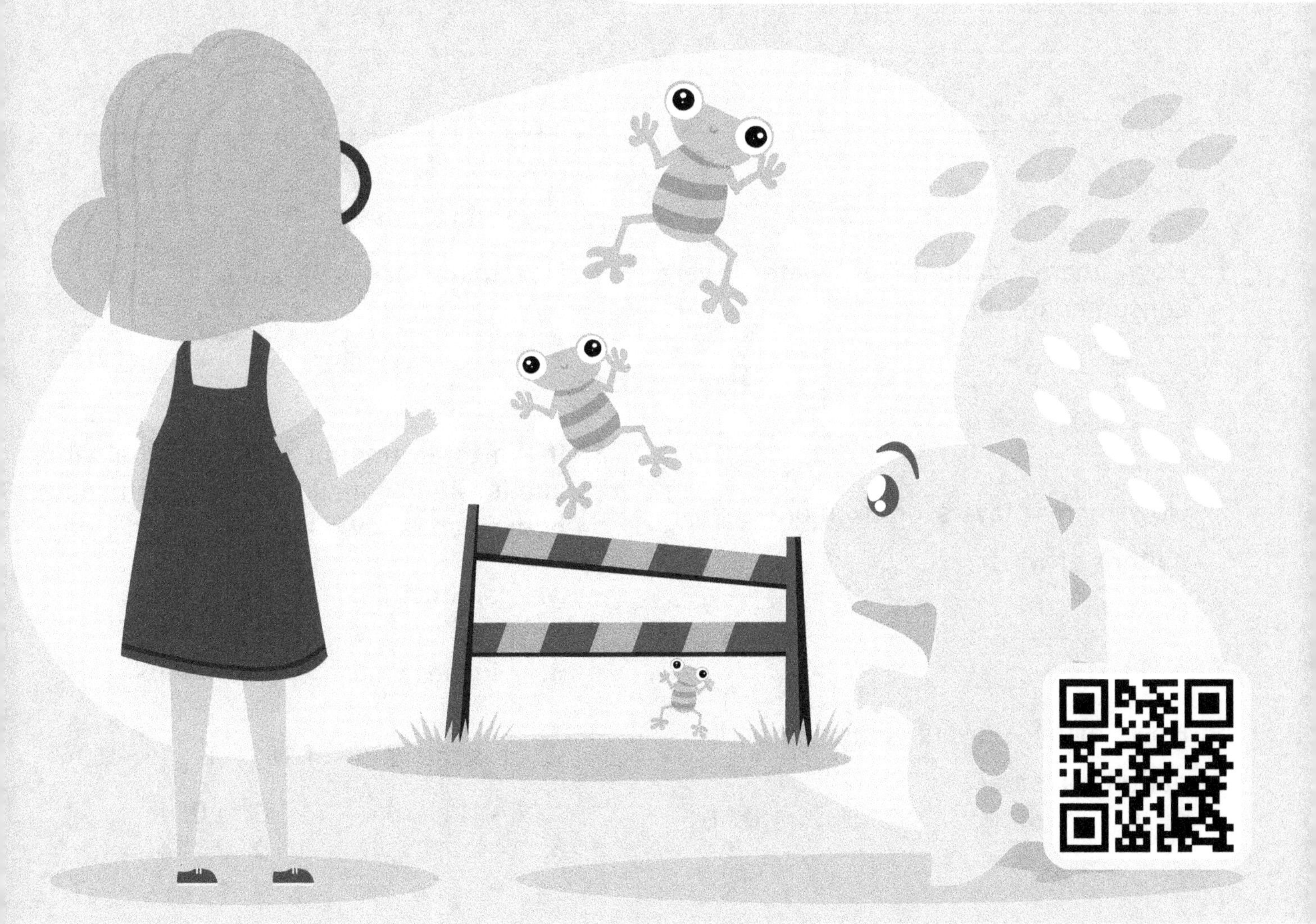

In Week 15 you will find lots of practice answering questions using sets of data. You will be reading dot plots to find information for real-world scenarios.

You can find detailed video explanations of each problem in the book by visiting: ArgoPrep.com

WEEK 15 : DAY 1

The amount of water that the tennis team drank on Tuesday is shown below. Use this information to answer questions 1 – 3.

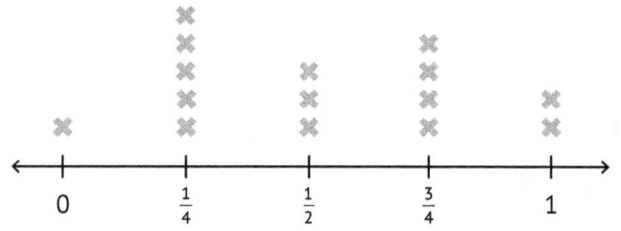

Below is a data set showing the rainfall on 12 days. Use this information to answer questions 4 – 5.

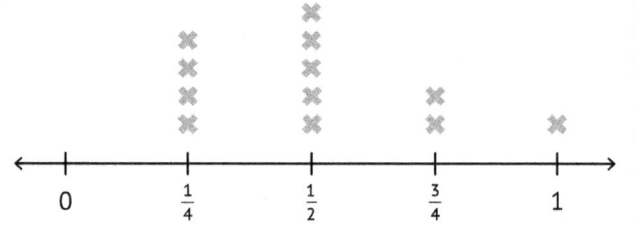

1. How many gallons of water were consumed in total?

   A. $6\frac{3}{8}$ B. $6\frac{7}{8}$ C. $7\frac{1}{4}$ D. $7\frac{3}{4}$

   5.MD.2

2. How many players drank more than $\frac{1}{4}$ gallons of water?

   A. 3 B. 5 C. 7 D. 9

   5.MD.2

3. How many players drank exactly $\frac{3}{4}$ gallons of water?

   A. 3 B. 4 C. 5 D. 6

   5.MD.2

4. How many inches of rain fell?

   A. 5 B. $5\frac{1}{8}$ C. $5\frac{1}{4}$ D. 6

   5.MD.2

5. If the total amount remained the same and it rained equally on each of the days, how much rain would there be on 1 day?

   A. $\frac{1}{2}$ an inch   C. 4 inches
   B. 2 inches   D. 8 inches

   5.MD.2

6. What is the value of 182 − 8 × (6 + 10)?

   A. 54   C. 1,054
   B. 144   D. 2,784

   5.OA.1

When looking at information given in charts or tables, look at ALL the clues given, not just the numbers but also the titles and units.

96

WEEK 15 : DAY 2

Robert measured some kudzu plants over a week. Their growth is shown below. Use this information to answer questions 1 – 2.

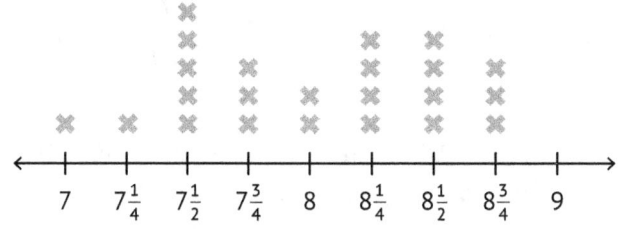

Kudzu Weekly Growth (feet)

1. How many plants did Robert measure?
   A. 5   B. 18   C. 23   D. 25

   5.MD.2

2. How many plants grew LESS than 8 feet that week?
   A. 2   B. 5   C. 7   D. 10

   5.MD.2

3. Which number can be written as $(1 \times 10{,}000) + (8 \times 100) + (4 \times 10) + (5 \times 1) + \left(3 \times \dfrac{1}{100}\right)$?

   A. 10,845.3
   B. 10,845.03
   C. 18,405.03
   D. 18,405.3

   5.NBT.3

The lengths of different branches were measured and the data is shown below. Use the information to answer questions 4 – 5.

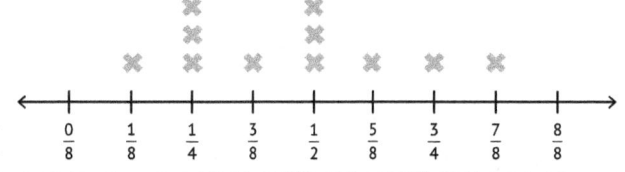

Length (feet)

4. If the branches were all laid end-to-end, how long would they stretch?
   A. 4 ft   B. 5 ft   C. 6 ft   D. 7 ft

   5.MD.2

5. If the combined length of the branches was the same but each branch was the same length as all the other branches, how long would each branch be?

   A. $\dfrac{2}{5}$ - foot   C. $\dfrac{1}{2}$ - foot

   B. $\dfrac{4}{11}$ - foot   D. $\dfrac{5}{11}$ - foot

   5.MD.2

6. How many $\dfrac{1}{3}$ - cup servings of cappuccino are in 10 cups of cappuccino?

   A. $3\dfrac{1}{3}$ B. 13   C. $15\dfrac{1}{3}$ D. 30

   5.NF.7

  TIP of the DAY

Each dot or "mark" on a plot represents 1 piece of information.

97

WEEK 15 : DAY 3

Some athletes' long jumps were recorded. Their distances are shown below. Use the information to answer questions 1 – 3.

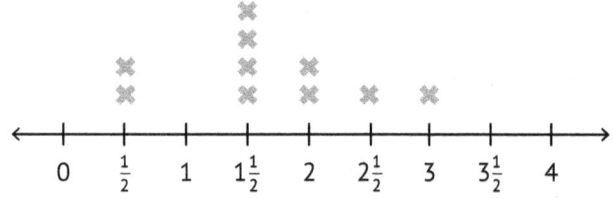

Distance jumped (meters)

1. What was the combined distance jumped by the athletes?

   A. $16\frac{1}{4}$ meters

   B. $16\frac{1}{2}$ meters

   C. $16\frac{3}{4}$ meters

   D. 7 meters

   5.MD.2

2. What was the distance most athletes jumped?

   A. $\frac{1}{2}$ of a meter

   B. $1\frac{1}{2}$ meters

   C. 2 meters

   D. $2\frac{1}{2}$ meters

   5.MD.2

3. If the total distance remained the same but each athlete jumped the same distance, how many meters would each athlete jump?

   A. $1\frac{3}{10}$ meters

   B. $1\frac{2}{5}$ meters

   C. $1\frac{13}{20}$ meters

   D. $1\frac{7}{10}$ meters

   5.MD.2

4. Which statement is true about the values of the two expressions below?

   Expression A: (54 × 72) – 3
   Expression B: 54 × 72

   A. The value of Expression A is 3 times the value of Expression B.

   B. The value of Expression B is 3 times the value of Expression A.

   C. The value of Expression A is 3 more than the value of Expression B.

   D. The value of Expression B is 3 more than the value of Expression A.

   5.OA.2

5. Look at 35.826. In a different number, the 6 represents a value which is ten times of the value of the 6 in 35.826. What value is represented by the 6 in the other number?

   A. six thousandths

   B. six hundredths

   C. six tenths

   D. six ones

   5NBT.1

TIP of the DAY

When adding or subtracting fractions (or mixed numbers), remember to make sure they have the same denominators first.

WEEK 15 : DAY 4

Below is some data about the amount of juice some first grade students drank. Use the data set to answer questions 1 – 3.

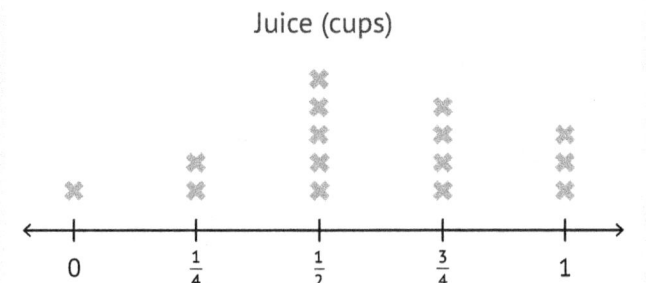

1. How much juice did the students drink on the day the data was recorded?

   A. 6 cups
   B. 9 cups
   C. 12 cups
   D. 15 cups

   5.MD.2

2. If all of the juice had been equally distributed to the students, how much juice would each student have received?

   A. $\frac{3}{5}$ - cup
   B. $\frac{1}{2}$ - cup
   C. $\frac{3}{4}$ - cup
   D. $\frac{4}{5}$ - cup

   5.MD.2

3. If the second grade class drank $2\frac{1}{3}$ times the amount of juice as the first grade class, how many cups of juice would the second graders drink?

   A. $11\frac{1}{3}$ cups
   B. $18\frac{1}{3}$ cups
   C. 21 cups
   D. 24 cups

   5.NF.6

Grandma Lemons measured the yearly growth of all of her grandchildren. The results are shown below. Use the information to answer questions 4.

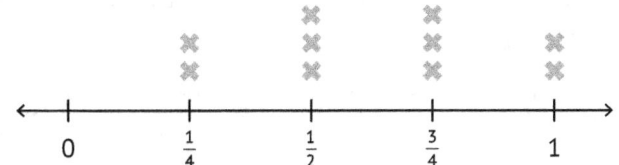

4. How many grandchildren does Grandma Lemons have?

   A. 4   B. 7   C. 10   D. 12

   5.MD.2

TIP of the DAY

Before taking tomorrow's assessment, make sure you understand how to read the data given.

99

WEEK 15 : DAY 5

ASSESSMENT

Ms. Leavey's class collected food for the local food bank. The contributions are shown below. Use the information to answer questions 1 – 3.

Food Donates (pounds)

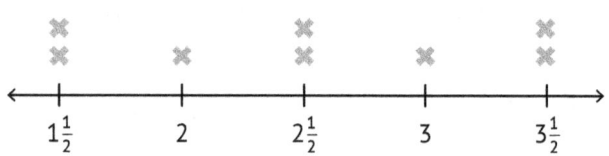

4. What is the area of the rectangle below?

   $\frac{1}{3}$ - foot

   $\frac{1}{8}$ - foot

   A. $\frac{1}{11}$ - ft^2 C. $\frac{1}{12}$ - ft^2

   B. $\frac{2}{11}$ - ft^2 D. $\frac{1}{24}$ - ft^2

   5.NF.4

1. How many students donated to the food bank?
   A. 4   B. 8   C. 12   D. 15

   5.MD.2

2. How many pounds of food did the class donate?
   A. 8   B. $12\frac{1}{2}$ C. $16\frac{1}{2}$ D. 20

   5.MD.2

3. If the amount collected was the same and everyone gave the same amount, how many pounds would each student give?
   A. $1\frac{1}{2}$ B. 2   C. $2\frac{1}{2}$ D. $3\frac{1}{2}$

   5.MD.2

5. Matilda earns $27 per hour. Over the course of 2 years she has worked 3,975 hours. How much money has Matilda earned in those 2 years?
   A. $107,325   C. $123,225
   B. $115,275   D. $214,650

   5.NBT.5

6. Which statement is true about the product of $\frac{4}{5} \times \frac{1}{3}$?
   A. The product is greater than each factor.
   B. The product is less than each factor.
   C. The product is greater than $\frac{1}{3}$ but less than $\frac{4}{5}$.
   D. The product is equal to one of the factors.

   5.NF.5

DAY 6 Challenge question

Nat ran 0.5 km on Monday, 2 km on Tuesday, and 4,600 m on Friday. How far did Nat run altogether?

5.MD.1

100

WEEK 16

VIDEO EXPLANATIONS

ARGOPREP.COM

Some people naturally do better when they can see three-dimensional shapes. Week 16's lessons have lots of practice finding the volume of three-dimensional figures.

You can find detailed video explanations to each problem in the book by visiting:
ArgoPrep.com

WEEK 16 : DAY 1

1. Opal filled a box with layers of unit cubes. The box had a volume of 360 cubic units. Which sentence about Opal's box must be true?

   A. There were 360 layers.
   B. There were 360 unit cubes per layer.
   C. There were 360 unit cubes that fit into the box exactly.
   D. The box held more than 360 unit cubes.

   5.MD.3

There were 4 different boxes that Oxana filled with unit cubes. The number of cubes used for the width, length and the number of layers are shown. Use this information to answer questions 3 – 5.

Box	Width	Length	Layers
A	2	2	16
B	3	12	4
C	9	4	6
D	4	4	4

2. How many unit cubes are in the box shown below?

   A. 6
   B. 10
   C. 15
   D. 30

   5.MD.3

3. Which box had the largest number of unit cubes?

   A. A   B. B   C. C   D. D

   5.MD.3

4. Which two boxes have the same number of unit cubes?

   A. A and B   C. B and C
   B. C and D   D. A and D

   5.MD.3

5. How many unit cubes were in Box B?

   A. 64   B. 144   C. 196   D. 216

   5.MD.3

TIP of the DAY

Volume is found by counting the number of unit cubes that can fit into a particular space.

WEEK 16 : DAY 2

1. How many unit cubes make up the box below?

   A. 12   B. 15   C. 60   D. 180

   5.MD.3

2. Quenton filled a box with layers of unit cubes. His box had a volume of 75 cubic units. Which sentence about Quenton's box must be true?

   A. There were 75 layers.
   B. There were 75 unit cubes per layer.
   C. The box had more than 75 unit cubes.
   D. There were 75 unit cubes that exactly fit into the box.

   5.MD.3

3. Sylvia was filling a box with unit cubes. She used 4 unit cubes for the width, 7 unit cubes for the length and it had 3 layers. How many unit cubes fit into the box?

   A. 14   B. 28   C. 42   D. 84

   5.MD.3

4. The raccoon weighs 6 pounds and 15 ounces. The turkey weighs 15 pounds 3 ounces. How much heavier is the turkey?

   A. $7\frac{3}{4}$ pounds   C. $8\frac{1}{4}$ pounds

   B. 8 pounds   D. $8\frac{1}{2}$ pounds

   5.MD.1

5. How many unit cubes fit in the box below?

   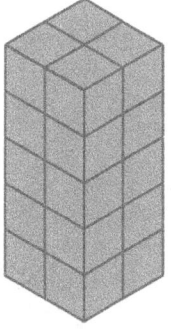

   A. 16   B. 20   C. 24   D. 40

   5.MD.3

TIP of the DAY

The number of unit cubes that fit into a space is the same number of cubic units that make up the volume of that same space.

103

WEEK 16 : DAY 3

There were 4 different boxes that were filled with unit cubes. The number of cubes used for the width, length and the number of layers are shown. Use this information to answer questions 1 - 3.

Box	Width	Length	Layers
A	10	2	12
B	4	12	8
C	8	11	6
D	4	6	9

1. How many unit cubes were in Box B?

   A. 184   B. 294   C. 384   D. 424

   5.MD.3

2. Which box has the most unit cubes in it?

   A. A   B. B   C. C   D. D

   5.MD.3

3. Which box has the fewest unit cubes in it?

   A. A   B. B   C. C   D. D

   5.MD.3

4. How many unit cubes make up the box below?

   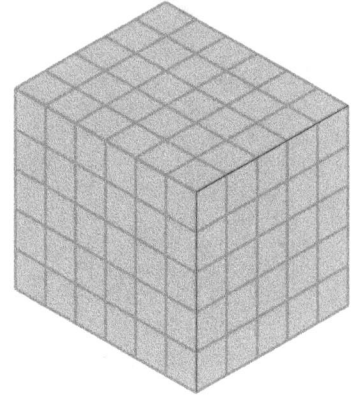

   A. 25
   B. 30
   C. 120
   D. 150

   5.MD.3

5. Perry filled a box with layers of unit cubes. The box had a volume of 155 cubic units. Which sentence about Perry's box must be true?

   A. There were 155 unit cubes that fit into the box exactly.
   B. The box had less than 155 unit cubes.
   C. There were 155 layers.
   D. There were 155 unit cubes per layer.

   5.MD.3

TIP of the DAY

Volume = length × width × height

WEEK 16 : DAY 4

1. Ruiz had a box that he completed and filled with exactly 210 unit cubes. Which sentence about Ruiz's box must be true?

   A. There were 210 layers.
   B. There were 210 unit cubes per layer.
   C. There were more than 210 unit cubes that could fit into the box.
   D. The box had a volume of 210 cubic units.

   5.MD.3

2. How many unit cubes are in the box below?

   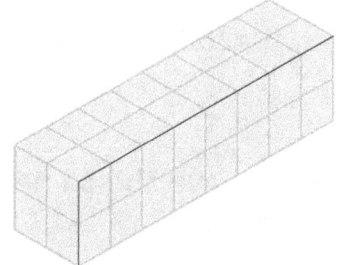

   A. 16   B. 32   C. 48   D. 64

   5.MD.3

3. Johnny was filling a box with unit cubes. He used 5 unit cubes for the width, 8 unit cubes for the length and it had 12 layers. How many unit cubes fit into the box?

   A. 96   B. 240   C. 480   D. 520

   5.MD.3

4. How many unit cubes are in the box below?

   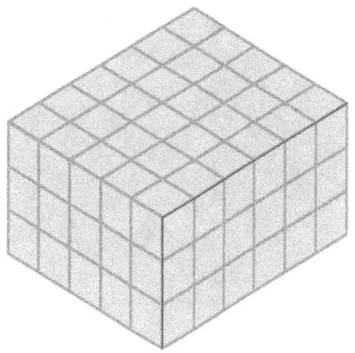

   A. 18   B. 50   C. 60   D. 90

   5.MD.3

5. Which statement is true?

   A. 19.8 > 19.697
   B. 135.07 < 134.981
   C. 468.101 = 468.011
   D. 58.32 > 58.4

   5.NBT.3

6. Roger was filling a box with unit cubes. He used 10 unit cubes for the width, 12 unit cubes for the length and it had 4 layers. How many unit cubes fit into the box?

   A. 240   B. 480   C. 590   D. 960

   5.MD.3

TIP of the DAY

The volume of a figure or prism represents the number of unit cubes that can fit into that space.

105

WEEK 16 : DAY 5

ASSESSMENT

1. How many cubes are in the box below?

   A. 6
   B. 12
   C. 18
   D. 24

   5.MD.3

2. Pria filled a box with layers of unit cubes. The box held exactly 425 unit cubes with no space leftover. Which sentence about Pria's box must be true?

   A. The box could hold more than 425 unit cubes.
   B. The volume of the box was 425 cubic units.
   C. There were 425 unit cubes per layer.
   D. There were 425 layers.

   5.MD.3

There were 4 different boxes that were filled with unit cubes. The number of cubes used for the width, length and the number of layers are shown. Use this information to answer questions 3 – 4.

Box	Width	Length	Layers
A	7	5	11
B	5	11	7
C	12	13	2

3. How many unit cubes were in Box C?

   A. 232   B. 262   C. 312   D. 372

   5.MD.3

4. Which boxes have the same number of unit cubes in them?

   A. A and B   C. A and D
   B. C and D   D. B and C

   5.MD.3

5. Jorge was filling a box with unit cubes. He used 5 unit cubes for the width, 10 unit cubes for the length and it had 4 layers. How many unit cubes fit into the box?

   A. 19   B. 54   C. 145   D. 200

   5.MD.3

DAY 6
Challenge question

One box holds exactly 250 unit cubes. What could its length, width and number of layers be?

5.MD.3

WEEK 17

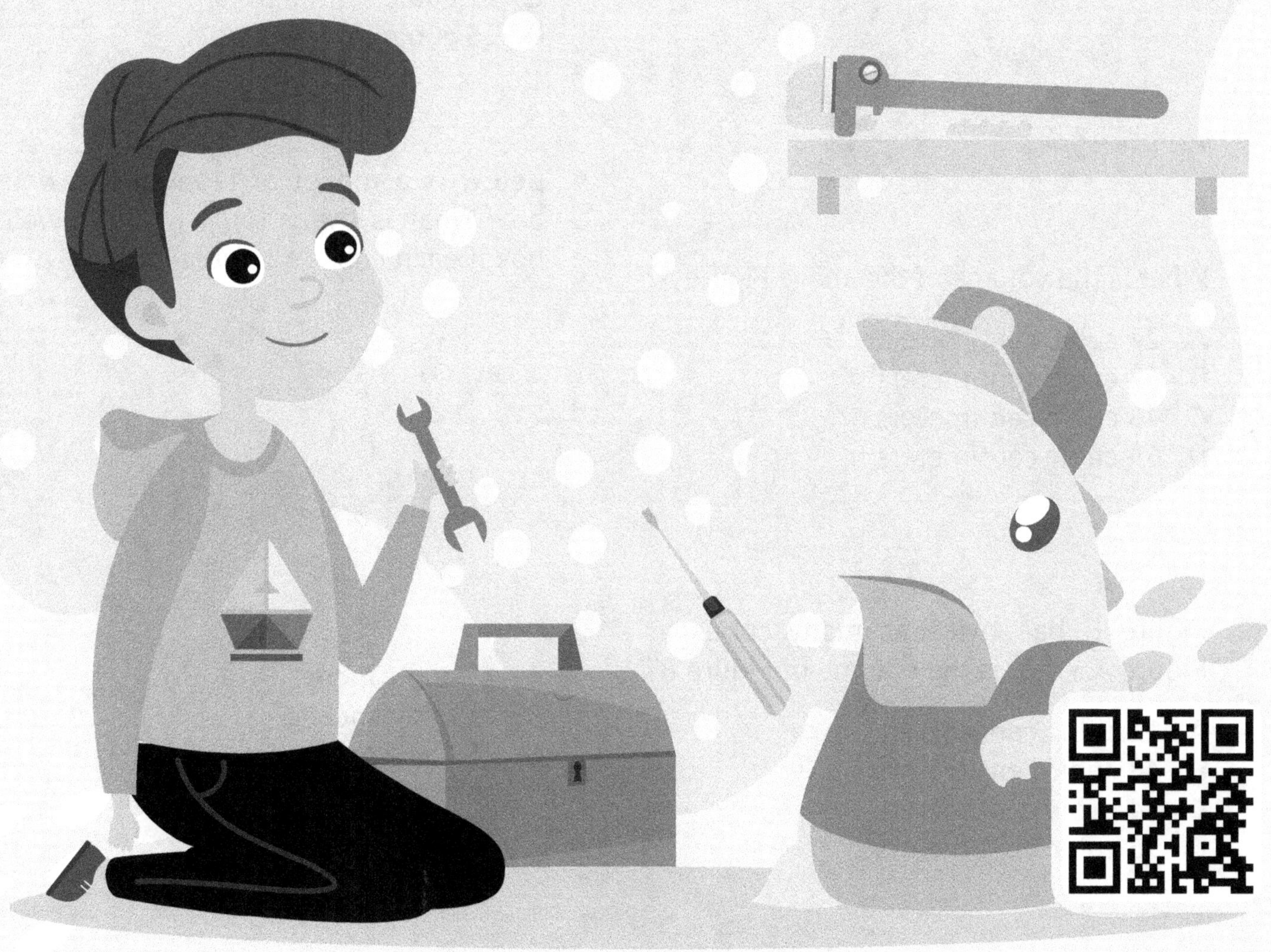

Week 17 goes further into the concept of volume and comparing the volumes of two or more figures.

You can find detailed video explanations of each problem in the book by visiting: ArgoPrep.com

WEEK 17 : DAY 1

Figure A is shown below. Each cube in Figure A is 1 cm³. Use the drawing to answer questions 1 – 3.

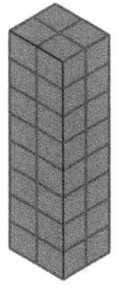

Figure A

1. What is the volume of the above Figure A?

   A. 24 cubic centimeters
   B. 32 cubic centimeters
   C. 48 cubic centimeters
   D. 64 cubic centimeters

   5.MD.4

2. Figure B has twice as many cubes as Figure A. What is the volume of Figure B?

   A. 12 cubic centimeters
   B. 48 cubic centimeters
   C. 64 cubic centimeters
   D. 96 cubic centimeters

   5.MD.4

3. Figure C has $\frac{1}{4}$ the number of cubes as Figure A. What is the volume of Figure C?

   A. 6 cubic centimeters
   B. 8 cubic centimeters
   C. 12 cubic centimeters
   D. 16 cubic centimeters

   5.MD.4

4. Below is a model of Monique's jewelry box. What is the volume of the jewelry box if each cube is 1 cubic inch?

   A. 15 cubic inches
   B. 21 cubic inches
   C. 25 cubic inches
   D. 30 cubic inches

   5.MD.4

TIP of the DAY

Volume is measured in cubic units.

WEEK 17 : DAY 2

Figure D is shown below and each cube is equal to 1 cubic inch. Use the drawing to answer questions 1 – 3.

Figure D

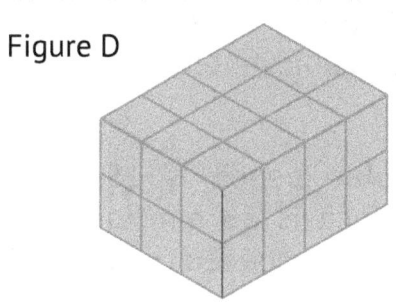

3. Figure F has 4 times the number of cubes as Figure D. What is the volume of Figure F?

   A. 64 cubic inches
   B. 96 cubic inches
   C. 104 cubic inches
   D. 256 cubic inches

   5.MD.4

Use the shoebox shown below to answer question 4. Each cube is 1 in³.

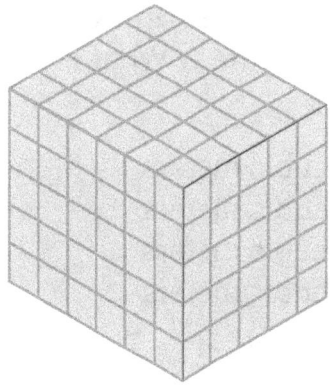

1. Figure E has $\frac{2}{3}$ the number of cubes as Figure D. What is the volume of Figure E?

   A. 6 cubic inches
   B. 8 cubic inches
   C. 12 cubic inches
   D. 16 cubic inches

   5.MD.4

2. What is the volume of Figure D?

   A. 12 cubic inches
   B. 18 cubic inches
   C. 24 cubic inches
   D. 26 cubic inches

   5.MD.4

4. What is the volume of the shoebox?

   A. 150 in³
   B. 170 in³
   C. 750 in³
   D. 900 in³

   5.MD.4

TIP of the DAY

1 cubic inch = 1 inch × 1 inch × 1 inch = 1 in³

109

WEEK 17 : DAY 3

Figure G is shown below. Use it to answer questions 1 – 3.

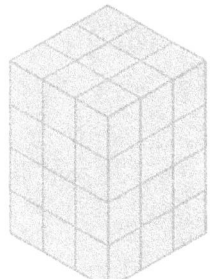

Figure G

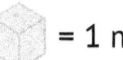 = 1 m³

1. Figure H has 9 times the number of cubes as Figure G. What is the volume of Figure H?

A. 108 cubic meters
B. 243 cubic meters
C. 324 cubic meters
D. 972 cubic meters

5.MD.4

2. Figure J has $\frac{1}{12}$ the number of cubes as Figure G. What is the volume of Figure J?

A. 3 cubic meters
B. 4 cubic meters
C. 9 cubic meters
D. 27 cubic meters

5.MD.4

3. What is the volume of Figure G?

A. 27 cubic meters
B. 36 cubic meters
C. 84 cubic meters
D. 108 cubic meters

5.MD.4

4. The blue pencil is 15 cm long. The red pencil is 86 mm long. What is the difference between the 2 pencils?

A. 64 mm   C. 71 mm
B. 64 cm   D. 71 cm

5.MD.1

5. Round 196,482.9105 to the nearest thousand.

A. 196,482.911
B. 196,482.91
C. 196,500
D. 196,000

5.NBT.4

6. What is the value of 200 + (6 × 18) − (10 ÷ 2)?

A. 149
B. 303
C. 1,849
D. 3,703

5.OA.1

TIP of the DAY

Volume is the space an object takes up. A milk jug is going to have a larger volume than a soda can because the jug takes up more space.

WEEK 17 : DAY 4

Figure K is shown below. Use the figure to answer questions 1 – 3.

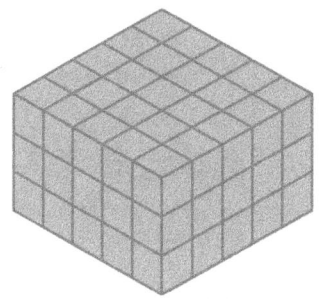

Figure K

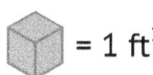 = 1 ft³

1. What is the volume of Figure K?

   A. 25 cubic feet
   B. 75 cubic feet
   C. 125 cubic feet
   D. 375 cubic feet

   5.MD.4

2. Figure L has a volume that is $\frac{1}{3}$ as large as Figure K. What is the volume of Figure L?

   A. 25 cubic feet
   B. 42 cubic feet
   C. 125 cubic feet
   D. 285 cubic feet

   5.MD.4

3. Figure M has a volume that is twice as large as Figure K. What is the volume of Figure M?

   A. 37.5 cubic feet
   B. 50 cubic feet
   C. 125 cubic feet
   D. 150 cubic feet

   5.MD.4

4. Which standard number is the same as fourteen thousand seven and eight thousandths?

   A. 40,007.08   C. 40,007.008
   B. 14,007.08   D. 14,007.008

   5.NBT.3

5. What is the volume for the rectangular prism below if each cube is 1 mm³?

   A. 63 mm³   C. 90 mm³
   B. 75 mm³   D. 105 mm³³

   5.MD.4

TIP of the DAY

Remember the connection between the number of unit cubes in a space and the volume of that space.

111

WEEK 17 : DAY 5

ASSESSMENT

Below is a box that is in Ryan's closet. Use the drawing to answer questions 1 – 3.

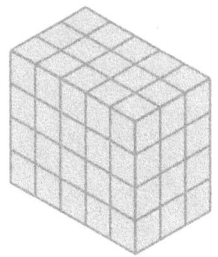

= 1 cm³

1. How much space does the box occupy?

   A. 48 cm³   C. 75 cm³
   B. 60 cm³   D. 80 cm³

   5.MD.4

2. How much space would 3 of these boxes occupy?

   A. 180 cm³   C. 240 cm³
   B. 225 cm³   D. 280 cm³   5.MD.4

3. Rhoda has a box that is $\frac{2}{5}$ as large as Ryan's box. What is the volume of Rhoda's box?

   A. 12 cm³   C. 24 cm³
   B. 18 cm³   D. 150 cm³   5.MD.4

Use the figure below to answer questions 4 – 6.

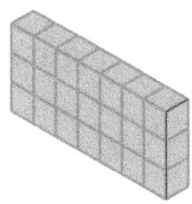

= 1 cm³

4. How many unit cubes are in the rectangular prism?

   A. 10   B. 18   C. 21   D. 24

   5.MD.3

5. If the figure above were laid flat to become the bottom layer of a rectangular prism that had 6 layers, what would the volume of the new rectangular prism be?

   A. 105 cm³   C. 141 cm³
   B. 126 cm³   D. 192 cm³   5.MD.4

6. What would be the volume of a rectangular prism that was $\frac{5}{7}$ of the volume of the original rectangular prism?

   A. 15 cm³   C. 24 cm³
   B. 18 cm³   D. 28 cm³   5.MD.4

DAY 6
Challenge question

There are 4 rectangular prisms that have a TOTAL volume of 288 cubic meters. If there was a box that was $\frac{1}{8}$ the size of one of the original boxes, what would its volume be?

5.MD.5

WEEK 18

VIDEO EXPLANATIONS

Volume, volume and more volume problems are found in Week 18. Be sure to use the correct units - some problems talk about area and others talk about volume.

You can find detailed video explanations of each problem in the book by visiting: ArgoPrep.com

WEEK 18 : DAY 1

1. What is the volume of the rectangular prism shown below?

   A. 20 in³
   B. 40 in³
   C. 72 in³
   D. 96 in³

   5.MD.5

2. There is a pool that is 5 feet deep and the area of the floor of the pool is 104 square feet. How much water would it take to fill that pool?

   A. 208 ft³
   B. 260 ft³
   C. 520 ft³
   D. 1,040 ft³

   5.MD.5

3. What multiplication equation is shown below?

   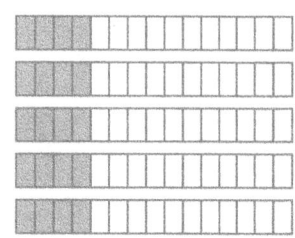

   A. $\frac{4}{15} \times 5 = 1\frac{1}{3}$
   B. $\frac{4}{15} \times 5 = 5\frac{4}{15}$
   C. $\frac{4}{15} \times 5 = 1\frac{11}{15}$
   D. $\frac{4}{15} \times 5 = \frac{3}{4}$

   5.NF.4

4. The shed had a floor that was 64 square feet and a height that was 9 feet. What was the volume of the shed?

   A. 288 ft³   C. 576 ft³
   B. 436 ft³   D. 720 ft³

   5.MD.5

Use the right rectangular prism below to answer questions 5 – 6.

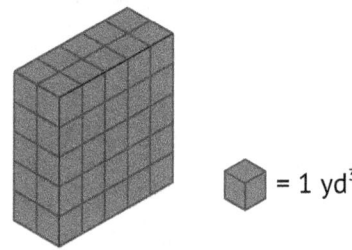

= 1 yd³

5. What is the volume of the prism?

   A. 40 yd³   C. 60 yd³
   B. 50 yd³   D. 75 yd³

   5.MD.5

6. If there was a different prism that had the same volume but a base of only 5 unit cubes, how many layers would the new prism have?

   A. 2   B. 5   C. 10   D. 20

   5.MD.5

TIP of the DAY

Volume is found by multiplying length × width × height.

114

WEEK 18 : DAY 2

1. What is the volume of the right rectangular prism shown?

   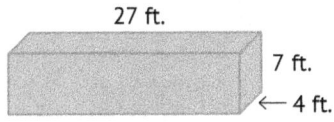

   A. 756 ft³
   B. 812 ft³
   C. 1,056 ft³
   D. 1,512 ft³

   5.MD.5

2. What is the volume of the right rectangular prism shown below?

   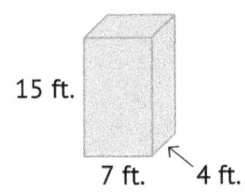

   A. 165 ft³
   B. 260 ft³
   C. 420 ft³
   D. 680 ft³

   5.MD.5

3. If the 2 boxes from #1 and #2 were joined together, what would be the volume of the new shape shown below?

   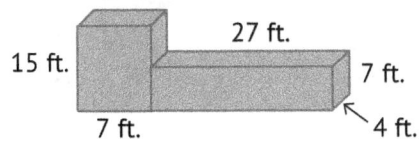

   A. 756 ft³
   B. 906 ft³
   C. 1,056 ft³
   D. 1,176 ft³

   5.MD.5

4. Look at the table below. Which statement is true?

Pattern A	Pattern B
1	3
2	6
3	9

   A. Pattern A's numbers are one-half of Pattern B's numbers.
   B. Pattern B has numbers that are 2 more than Pattern A's numbers.
   C. All of Pattern A's numbers will also be found in Pattern B.
   D. Pattern A has numbers that are one-third of Pattern B's numbers.

   5.OA.3

5. Timothy played golf for $5\frac{2}{3}$ hours. Terry played $1\frac{1}{2}$ times as much as Timothy. How many hours did Terry play golf?

   A. $7\frac{5}{6}$
   B. 8
   C. $8\frac{1}{3}$
   D. $8\frac{1}{2}$

   5.NF.6

TIP of the DAY

Volume takes up three-dimensional space so the units used to measure volume are cubic units, which are also three-dimensional.

115

WEEK 18 : DAY 3

1. There is a tank at the zoo that is 23 meters deep and the area of the floor of the tank is 468 meters². How much water is in that tank?

   A. 9,360 m³
   B. 10,764 m³
   C. 11,700 m³
   D. 12,364 m³

   5.MD.5

2. Figure A has a length of 5 yards, a width of 9 yards and depth of 2 yards. Figure B is shown below.

   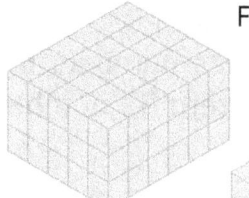

   Figure B

   = 1 yd³

   Which statement is true about the 2 rectangular prisms?

   A. The volumes of Figures A and B are equal.
   B. Figure A has a larger volume than Figure B by 10 cubic yards.
   C. Figure B has a larger volume than Figure A by 25 cubic yards.
   D. There is not enough information to find the volumes.

   5.MD.5

3. Figure N is 10 in³ larger than the prism below. What is the volume of the Figure N?

   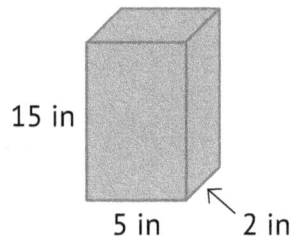

   15 in

   5 in   2 in

   A. 35 in³
   B. 85 in³
   C. 135 in³
   D. 160 in³

4. What is the area of the rectangle shown below?

   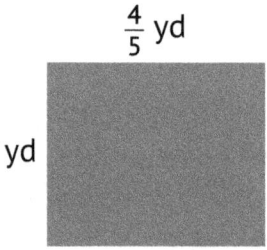

   $\frac{4}{5}$ yd

   $\frac{2}{3}$ yd

   A. $\frac{3}{8}$ yd²   C. $\frac{6}{15}$ yd²
   B. $\frac{6}{8}$ yd²   D. $\frac{8}{15}$ yd²

   5.NF.4

TIP of the DAY

Volumes can be added together. If Figure A is 45 m³ and Figure B is 16 m³, if you combine the Figures A and B, the new volume would be 61 m³.

116

WEEK 18 : DAY 4

1. A right rectangular prism has a volume of 210 cubic meters. If the height is 6 meters, which of the numbers could be the length?

   A. 2 meters
   B. 3 meters
   C. 5 meters
   D. 6 meters

   5.MD.5

2. There is a toolbox that could be completely filled with 106 unit cubes. Which sentence about the toolbox must be true?

   A. There are 106 layers.
   B. There are 106 unit cubes per layer.
   C. There are more than 106 unit cubes that could fit into the box.
   D. The box has a volume of 106 cubic units.

   5.MD.3

3. The Steed's fish tank is 18 inches tall and the area of the floor of the tank is 546 inches². How much water is in that tank when it is full?

   A. 9,720 in³
   B. 9,828 in³
   C. 10,920 in³
   D. 11,000 in³

   5.MD.5

Use the drawing below to answer questions 4 – 5.

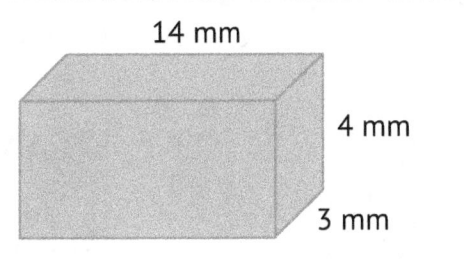

4. What is the volume of the prism above?

   A. 98 mm³
   B. 168 mm³
   C. 336 mm³
   D. 504 mm³

   5.MD.5

5. If 3 of the above prisms were connected together, what would be the volume of the new shape?

   A. 196 mm³
   B. 294 mm³
   C. 504 mm³
   D. 1,008 mm³

   5.MD.5

6. Which statement is true?

   A. 163.8 > 163.709
   B. 34.56 = 34.65
   C. 487.2 < 487.20
   D. 9.076 > 9.1

   5.NBT.3

TIP of the DAY

Volume can also be calculated by finding the area of the base of the prism and multiplying it by the height of the prism.

117

WEEK 18 : DAY 5

ASSESSMENT

The figures below are only the bases of right rectangular prisms that are all 8 feet in height. Figure A's base is a square. Use the drawing to answer questions 1 – 3.

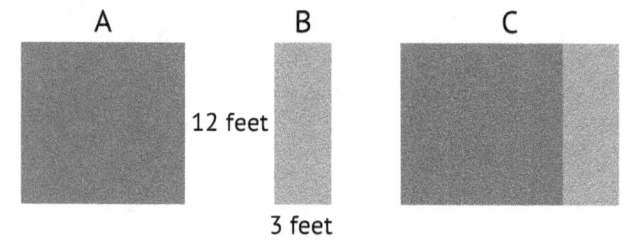

1. What is the volume of Figure A?

   A. 96 feet^3
   B. 192 feet^3
   C. 384 feet^3
   D. 1,152 feet^3

   5.MD.5

2. What is the volume of Figure B?

   A. 96 feet^3
   B. 120 feet^3
   C. 192 feet^3
   D. 288 feet^3

   5.MD.5

3. Figure C is formed by adding Figures A and B together. What is the volume of Figure C?

   A. 216 ft^3 C. 1,440 ft^3
   B. 1,248 ft^3 D. 2,880 ft^3

   5.MD.5

The table below has the dimensions for 4 different right rectangular prisms. Use the table to answer questions 4 – 5.

Prism	Length	Width	Height
A	18 cm	12 cm	5 cm
B	7 cm	10 cm	18 cm
C	12 cm	8 cm	9 cm
D	10 cm	18 cm	7 cm

4. Which 2 prisms have the same volume?

   A. A and B   C. A and C
   B. C and D   D. B and D

   5.MD.3

5. Which prism has the smallest volume?

   A. A   B. B   C. C   D. D

   5.MD.5

DAY 6
Challenge question

If all of the 4 prisms from the table above were joined together, what would the combined volume be?

5.MD.5

118

WEEK 19

This week (Week 19) you will learn how to graph points and find the coordinates of points on a graph.

You can find detailed video explanations of each problem in the book by visiting: ArgoPrep.com

WEEK 19 : DAY 1

Use the graph below to answer questions 1 – 5.

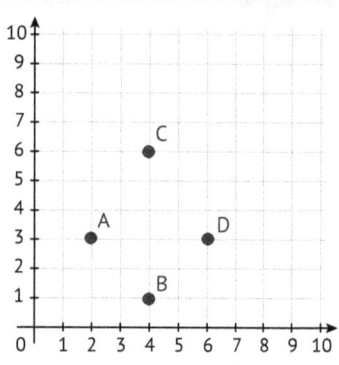

1. What are the coordinates for Point A?

   A. (3, 2) C. (3, 4)
   B. (2, 3) D. (4, 3)

   5.G.1

2. What is the x-coordinate for Point B?

   A. 1   B. 2   C. 4   D. 6

   5.G.1

3. Which 2 points have the same x-coordinate?

   A. A and B   C. A and D
   B. C and D   D. B and C

   5.G.1

4. Which 2 points have the same y-coordinate?

   A. A and B
   B. C and D
   C. A and D
   D. B and C

   5.G.1

5. Which point is located at (6, 3)?

   A. A
   B. B
   C. C
   D. D

   5.G.1

6. Which statement is true about the product of $\frac{4}{5} \times 6$?

   A. The product is greater than $\frac{4}{5}$ but less than 6.
   B. The product is less than each factor.
   C. The product is equal to one of the factors.
   D. The product is greater than each factor.

   5.NF.5

TIP of the DAY

The order of the coordinates of an ordered pair is very important. If the order changes, the location of the point changes.

120

WEEK 19 : DAY 2

Use the graph below to answer questions 1 – 4.

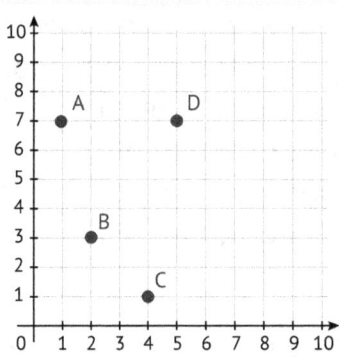

1. What is the y-coordinate for Point C?

   A. 1
   B. 2
   C. 4
   D. 5

   5.G.1

2. What are the coordinates for Point D?

   A. (7, 4)
   B. (4, 7)
   C. (7, 5)
   D. (5, 7)

   5.G.1

3. Which 2 points have the same y-coordinate?

   A. A and B
   B. C and D
   C. A and D
   D. B and C

   5.G.1

4. Which point is located at (2, 3)?

   A. A
   B. B
   C. C
   D. D

   5.G.1

5. What are the coordinates for the origin?

   A. (7, 7)
   B. (4, 4)
   C. (1, 1)
   D. (0, 0)

   5.G.1

6. What is the product of 3.19 and 10^3?

   A. 3,190
   B. 319
   C. 3.19000
   D. 0.00319

   5.NBT.2

TIP of the DAY

The first coordinate in an ordered pair is the x-coordinate. The x-coordinate shows the horizontal distance from the origin.

WEEK 19 : DAY 3

The table and graph below represent 4 trees in a forest. Use the information to answer questions 1 – 4.

Tree	Point on Graph
Apple	A
Beech	B
Cherry	C
Dogwood	D

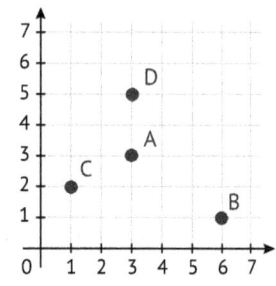

1. Where is the Beech tree located?

   A. (6, 1) C. (3, 5)
   B. (1, 6) D. (5, 3)

   5.G.2

2. What is the y-coordinate for the Cherry tree?

   A. 1   B. 2   C. 4   D. 6

   5.G.2

3. Which statement is true about the Apple and Dogwood trees?

   A. They have the same y-coordinate.
   B. They have the same x-coordinate.
   C. The y-coordinate of A is larger than the y-coordinate of D.
   D. The x-coordinate of D is larger than the x-coordinate of A.

   5.G.2

4. Which tree is closest to (1, 3)?

   A. Apple
   B. Birch
   C. Cherry
   D. Dogwood

   5.G.2

5. Which number has a 5 that is $\frac{1}{100}$ the value of the 5 in 6,485.92?

   A. 2,507.3
   B. 42,956.08
   C. 931.57
   D. 1,642.951

   5.NBT.1

TIP of the DAY

The second coordinate in an ordered pair is the y-coordinate. The y-coordinate shows the vertical distance from the origin.

122

WEEK 19 : DAY 4

The table and graph below represent 4 products in a store. Use the information to answer questions 1 – 3.

Product	Point on Graph
Avocados	A
Bananas	B
Cereal	C
Donuts	D

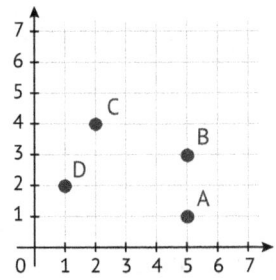

1. Where is the cereal located?

   A. (5, 1)   C. (4, 2)
   B. (1, 2)   D. (2, 4)

   5.G.2

2. The milk is located at (4, 1). Which product is closest to the milk?

   A. Avocados   C. Cereal
   B. Bananas   D. Donuts

   5.G.2

3. Which statement is true about the products shown on the graph?

   A. The avocados and bananas have the same y-coordinate.
   B. The cereal has the largest x-coordinate.
   C. The bananas and avocados are closer to each other than any other 2 products.
   D. The donuts are located at (2, 1).

   5.G.2

4. What is 51 × 4,068?

   A. 23,868   C. 197,968
   B. 173,568   D. 207,468

   5.NBT.5

5. Grandma Jeanne painted for 6 hours. Her grandson painted with her for $\frac{5}{12}$ of that time. How much time did Grandma Jeanne spend with her grandson painting?

   A. more than 6 hours
   B. less than 6 hours
   C. less than $\frac{5}{12}$ of an hour
   D. exactly $\frac{5}{12}$ of an hour

   5.NF.5

When using ordered pairs, remember to always begin at the origin (0, 0).

123

WEEK 19 : DAY 5

ASSESSMENT

The table and graph below represent 4 locations of restaurants. Use the information to answer questions 1 – 4.

Restaurant	Point on Graph
A. Eatz	A
Big Al's	B
Chops	C
The Diner	D

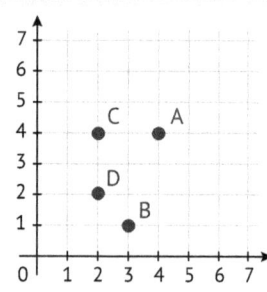

1. Which 2 restaurants are located the closest to each other?
   A. Big Al's and A. Eatz
   B. Chops and The Diner
   C. The Diner and Big Al's
   D. Chops and A. Eatz

   5.G.2

2. What are the coordinates for Chops?
   A. (2, 4)   C. (2, 2)
   B. (1, 2)   D. (3, 1)

   5.G.2

3. Which statement is NOT true about the locations of the restaurants?
   A. Chops is the same distance from The Diner and from A. Eatz.
   B. Chops and A. Eatz have the same x-coordinate.
   C. Big Al's has the smallest y-coordinate.
   D. The Diner is located at (2, 2).

   5.G.2

4. A parking lot is located at (4, 2). Which restaurant is closest to the parking lot?
   A. Eatz   C. Chopin
   B. Big Al's   D. The Diner

   5.G.2

5. What is the volume of a right rectangular prism that can fit 5 more cubes into it than the right rectangular prism shown below?

    = 1 ft³

   A. 45 ft³   C. 55 ft³
   B. 50 ft³   D. 60 ft³

   5.MD.5

DAY 6 Challenge question

Point A is located at (3, 5). Point B has the same x-coordinate and is 5 units from Point A, what is the ordered pair for Point B?

5.G.1

124

Last week - way to go! Week 20 gives lots of exercises to help you understand attributes and traits that are given to specific shapes.

You can find detailed video explanations of each problem in the book by visiting: ArgoPrep.com

WEEK 20 : DAY 1

1. Which shape does NOT have 4 sides?

    A. trapezoid
    B. rhombus
    C. quadrilateral
    D. pentagon

2. Which statement is true?

    A. An equilateral triangle has only 1 pair of parallel lines.
    B. All hexagons have 8 sides.
    C. All rhombuses are parallelograms.
    D. Parallelograms have 2 pairs of right angles.

3. Which shape has 5 sides?

    A. parallelogram
    B. pentagon
    C. hexagon
    D. octagon

4. Which statement is NOT true?

    A. All trapezoids are quadrilaterals.
    B. All triangles have 3 sides.
    C. All quadrilaterals have 4 sides.
    D. All rectangles are squares.

5. Which of the following triangles have 3 sides that are the same length?

    A. scalene triangle
    B. isosceles triangle
    C. equilateral triangle
    D. obtuse triangle

6. Victoria has a rectangle. What is NOT true about rectangles?

    A. Rectangles have 4 sides that are equal.
    B. Rectangles have only right angles.
    C. Rectangles have 2 pairs of parallel lines.
    D. Rectangles are quadrilaterals.

TIP of the DAY

Shapes may fit into more than one category or have more than one description. For example, a square is a quadrilateral and it is an equilateral.

WEEK 20 : DAY 2

1. Which shape is three-sided and has exactly 2 equal sides?

   A. scalene triangle
   B. isosceles triangle
   C. equilateral triangle
   D. obtuse triangle

2. Which shape has 4 equal sides but no right angles?

   A. square
   B. rectangle
   C. rhombus
   D. trapezoid

3. Kara has a shape that has 8 sides and 4 pairs of parallel lines. What is Kara's shape?

   A. parallelogram
   B. pentagon
   C. hexagon
   D. octagon

4. Which shape below does NOT have any parallel sides?

   A. isosceles triangle
   B. square
   C. trapezoid
   D. rhombus

5. Will has an equilateral triangle. What is NOT true about equilateral triangles?

   A. Equilateral triangles have 3 acute angles.
   B. Equilateral triangles have 3 sides.
   C. Equilateral triangles have exactly 1 obtuse angle.
   D. Equilateral triangles have sides that are equal.

6. There is a block of concrete that weighs 12 pounds and 5 ounces. There is also a bag of sand that weighs 20 pounds and 1 ounce. How much heavier is the sand?

   A. $7\frac{1}{4}$ pounds
   B. $7\frac{1}{2}$ pounds
   C. $7\frac{3}{4}$ pounds
   D. $7\frac{2}{4}$ pounds

This is your last week in this workbook – finish strong!

WEEK 20 : DAY 3

1. There is a shape that is a quadrilateral with exactly 1 pair of parallel lines. What is the shape?

   A. parallelogram
   B. square
   C. rhombus
   D. trapezoid

   5.G.4

2. There is a shape that is a quadrilateral with 2 pairs of parallel lines. What shape is NOT being described?

   A. pentagon
   B. square
   C. rhombus
   D. parallelogram

   5.G.4

Use the drawing below to answer questions 3 – 4.

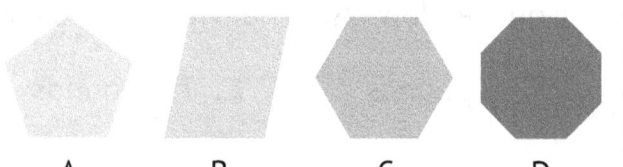

A   B   C   D

3. Which of the shapes is a parallelogram?

   A. A   B. B   C. C   D. D

   5.G.3

4. Which 2 shapes appear to have only pairs of parallel lines and are equilateral?

   A. A and B   C. A and C
   B. C and D   D. B and D

   5.G.3

5. Vince had a shape that had exactly 1 pair of parallel lines and 4 sides. What was Vince's shape?

   A. trapezoid
   B. parallelogram
   C. kite
   D. rhombus

   5.G.4

6. What is the value of $14\frac{3}{5} + 13\frac{4}{8}$?

   A. $27\frac{1}{10}$ C. $28\frac{1}{10}$
   B. $27\frac{7}{10}$ D. $28\frac{9}{10}$

   5.NF.1

TIP of the DAY

When a description says "EXACTLY" that means no more and no less, so if there is EXACTLY 1 pair of parallel lines, there are not 2 or 3 pairs, there is ONE pair.

128

WEEK 20 : DAY 4

Use the drawing below to answer questions 1 – 2.

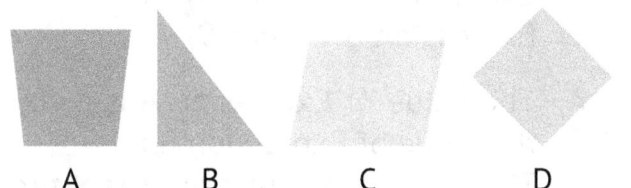

A   B   C   D

1. Which shape is NOT a quadrilateral?

A. A
B. B
C. C
D. D

5.G.4

2. Which 2 shapes are parallelograms?

A. A and C
B. B and D
C. A and B
D. C and D

5.G.4

3. Yolanda had a shape that has 4 sides that are equal. Which shape could be Yolanda's?

A. rhombus
B. triangle
C. trapezoid
D. pentagon

5.G.4

4. Which statement about rhombuses is NOT true?

A. Rhombuses have 4 sides.
B. Rhombuses have equal sides.
C. Opposite angles on a rhombus are equal.
D. Rhombuses have 4 right angles.

5.G.4

5. How many $\frac{1}{5}$ - gallons are in 5 gallons?

A. 1
B. 5
C. 25
D. 50

5.NF.7

TIP of the DAY

Before tomorrow's assessment (and the final one at the end), make sure you are clear on what attributes are required for a certain shape or shape category.

129

WEEK 20 : DAY 5

ASSESSMENT

1. Figure Z has 3 angles and 1 of them is obtuse. What is Figure Z?

   A. quadrilateral
   B. isosceles triangle
   C. equilateral triangle
   D. obtuse triangle

   5.G.4

2. In which category do ALL of the shapes below belong?

   A   B   C   D

   A. squares
   B. parallelograms
   C. quadrilaterals
   D. rhombuses

   5.G.4

3. What do rectangles and squares NOT have in common?

   A. 4 right angles
   B. opposite sides are parallel
   C. 4 sides
   D. all sides are equal

   5.G.4

4. Which statement is true about the values of the two expressions below?

   Expression A: (5 × 9) − 8
   Expression B: (5 × 9)

   A. The value of Expression A is 8 times the value of Expression B.
   B. The value of Expression B is 8 times the value of Expression A.
   C. The value of Expression A is 8 more than the value of Expression B.
   D. The value of Expression B is 8 more than the value of Expression A.

   5.NF.5

5. Scarlett uses $8\frac{1}{3}$ pounds of tomatoes per recipe of red sauce. How many pounds of tomatoes would she need to make 7 batches of red sauce?

   A. $56\frac{1}{3}$ C. $58\frac{1}{3}$

   B. $57\frac{2}{3}$ D. $58\frac{2}{3}$

   5.NF.6

DAY 6
Challenge question

List all of the attributes that squares and rhombuses have in common.

5.G.4

Great job finishing all 20 weeks! You should be ready for any test.

Try this assessment to see how much you've learned - good luck!

ASSESSMENT

1. The number 57.209 is given. In a different number, the 2 represents a value which is one-tenth of the value of the 2 in 57.206. What value is represented by the 2 in the other number?

   A. two hundredths
   B. two tenths
   C. two ones
   D. two tens

   5.NBT.1

2. Which term can be put in the blank to make the statement true?

   500,000 = 50 _____

   A. thousands
   B. ten-thousands
   C. hundred-thousands
   D. millions

   5.NBT.1

3. Which number is equal to three hundred twelve and thirteen hundredths?

   A. 312.13
   B. 312.013
   C. 3012.13
   D. 30012.13

   5.NBT.3

4. The results of a survey of 5th graders who take music lessons is shown below.

Violin	$\frac{1}{4}$
Piano	$\frac{1}{3}$
Trumpet	$\frac{1}{12}$

   What fraction of the 5th graders play something OTHER than the 3 instruments listed?

   A. $\frac{1}{2}$ B. $\frac{1}{3}$ C. $\frac{1}{4}$ D. $\frac{1}{12}$

   5.NF.2

5. Which mathematical expression is equivalent to the number sentence below?

   Subtract 7 from 12, and then multiply by 9.

   A. 7 − 12 × 9   C. 12 − 7 × 9
   B. 7 − (12 × 9)   D. (12 − 7) × 9

   5.OA.2

6. Someone put 22 kilograms of vegetables evenly into 12 bags. How many kilograms of vegetables will be in each bag?

   A. $1\frac{1}{12}$ C. $1\frac{5}{6}$
   B. $1\frac{3}{6}$ D. $1\frac{5}{12}$

   5.NF.3

134

ASSESSMENT

7. A piece of material is 0.587 yards long. Round 0.587 to the nearest tenth.

   A. 1.0
   B. 0.6
   C. 0.59
   D. 0.587

   5.NBT.4

8. Which statement is true about the values of the two expressions below?

   Expression A: 4 × (33 + 8)
   Expression B: (33 + 8)

   A. The value of Expression A is 4 times the value of Expression B.
   B. The value of Expression B is 4 times the value of Expression A.
   C. The value of Expression A is 4 more than the value of Expression B.
   D. The value of Expression B is 4 more than the value of Expression A.

   5.OA.2

9. Mrs. Dreher cut a 33-foot piece of twine into 12 equal pieces for wrapping gifts. How long was each piece of twine?

   A. $2\frac{7}{12}$ feet
   B. $2\frac{2}{3}$ feet
   C. $2\frac{1}{2}$ feet
   D. $2\frac{3}{4}$ feet

   5.NF.3

10. Which scenario could be described by the model below?

    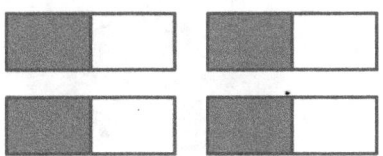

    A. Zara drank $\frac{1}{2}$ a gallon of juice each day for 4 days.
    B. Ivor mowed 4 lawns on 2 different weeks.
    C. Shana walked 4 miles in $\frac{1}{2}$ a minute.
    D. Warren worked $\frac{1}{2}$ a day Monday - Wednesday.

    5.NF.4

11. Which statement is true about the product of $\frac{6}{5} \times \frac{3}{4}$?

    A. The product is greater than each factor.
    B. The product is less than each factor.
    C. The product is greater than $\frac{3}{4}$ but less than $\frac{6}{5}$.
    D. The product is equal to one of the factors.

    5.NF.5

ASSESSMENT

12. How many unit cubes are in the box shown below?

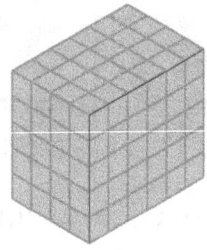

   A. 70
   B. 90
   C. 100
   D. 120

   5.MD.5

13. There are two number patterns below.

   Pattern A: 0, 1, 2, 3, 4...
   Pattern B: 0, 2, 4, 6, 8...

   Which statement is true about the patterns?

   A. All of the numbers in the 2 patterns are different.
   B. All of the numbers in Pattern A can be found in Pattern B.
   C. The 6th number in Pattern B is 2 times as large as the 6th number in Pattern A.
   D. The numbers in Pattern B are half the value of the numbers in Pattern A.

   5.OA.3

14. Which statement about rectangles is NOT true?

   A. Rectangles are parallelograms.
   B. Rectangles have 4 equal sides.
   C. Opposite sides on a rectangle are equal.
   D. Rectangles have 4 right angles.

   5.G.4

15. There is a kiddie pool that is 2.5 meters deep and the area of the floor of the pool is 96 square meters. How much water would it take to fill that pool?

   A. 192 m^3
   B. 240 m^3
   C. 282 m^3
   D. 310 m^3

   5.MD.5

16. What is the value of the expression below?

   $$13 + 2(10 - 6 \div 2) \div 2$$

   A. 8.5
   B. 15
   C. 20
   D. 52.5

   5.OA.1

17. Which expression is the same as 8×10^5?

   A. 800,000
   B. 80,000
   C. 8,000
   D. 800

   5.NBT.2

136

ASSESSMENT

18. $10\frac{3}{4} + 11\frac{7}{8} = ?$

   A. $21\frac{10}{12}$
   C. $22\frac{5}{8}$
   B. $22\frac{10}{12}$
   D. $23\frac{1}{8}$

   5.NF.1

19. What is the value of the expression: $15 \div \frac{1}{3}$?

   A. $\frac{1}{5}$ B. $\frac{1}{45}$ C. 5 D. 45

   5.NF.7

20. The bear cub weighed 45 pounds and 13 ounces. How many ounces did the bear weigh?

   A. 58 C. 733
   B. 585 D. 913

   5.MD.1

21. Which equation could be shown by the model below?

   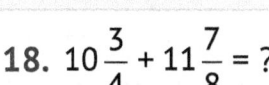

   A. 24 × 6 = 4 C. 30 − 6 = 24
   B. 24 + 6 = 30 D. 24 ÷ 6 = 4

   5.NBT.6

22. Which shape does NOT have at least 1 pair of parallel lines?

   A. rectangle
   B. parallelogram
   C. equilateral triangle
   D. trapezoid

   5.G.3

23. Which number is the product of 815 and 106?

   A. 13,040
   B. 86,390
   C. 105,980
   D. 128,800

   5.NBT.5

24. Which equation is NOT shown in the model below?

   A. 5 × 5 × 3 = 75
   B. 15 × 5 = 75
   C. 75 ÷ 5 = 15
   D. 15 + 3 = 18

   5.NBT.6

137

ASSESSMENT

25. Wyatt studied for $2\frac{1}{2}$ hours last week. Zooey studied $4\frac{1}{5}$ times as long. Which equation could be used to find out how many hours Zooey studied last week?

   A. $2\frac{1}{2} \times 4\frac{1}{5} = 8\frac{1}{10}$

   B. $2\frac{1}{2} \times 4\frac{1}{5} = 10\frac{1}{2}$

   C. $2\frac{1}{2} \times 4\frac{1}{5} = 6\frac{1}{10}$

   D. $2\frac{1}{2} \times 4\frac{1}{5} = 10\frac{1}{10}$

   5.NF.6

26. Which point can be found by moving 2 units to the right on the x-axis and 5 units up on the y-axis?

   A. (2, 5)
   B. (5, 2)
   C. (2x, 5y)
   D. (2/5)

   5.G.1

27. Which equation can be used to find the value of the expression below?

   $$72.15 + 96.3$$

   A. 72.15 × 96.3 = 6948.05
   B. 72.15 + 96.3 = 81.78
   C. 72.15 + 96.3 = 817.8
   D. 168.45 − 72.15 = 96.3

   5.NBT.4

Use the dot plot below to answer questions 28 – 29. It shows the rainfall recorded over 1 week.

Rainfall (inches)

28. How much total rainfall was there during the week recorded?

   A. 2 inches
   B. $2\frac{1}{2}$ inches
   C. $2\frac{3}{4}$ inches
   D. 3 inches

   5.MD.2

29. If that week had the same amount of rainfall, but it rained the same amount each day, how much rain would fall per day?

   A. $\frac{1}{7}$ of an inch
   B. $\frac{2}{7}$ of an inch
   C. $\frac{3}{7}$ of an inch
   D. $2\frac{1}{3}$ inches

   5.MD.2

ASSESSMENT

The table below shows the animals in a zoo and the point that corresponds to each animal. Use the table and graph below to answer questions 30 – 32.

Aardvark	A
Bear	B
Cougar	C
Deer	D
Emu	E

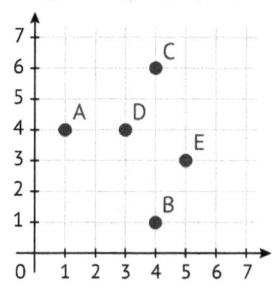

30. What are the coordinates for Point E?
_____
_____

5.G.1

31. Which 2 animals have the same x-coordinate?
_____
_____

5.G.1

32. The zookeeper is at (1, 2) on the graph. Which animal is closest to the keeper?
_____
_____

5.G.2

33. Looking at the shapes below, list ALL of the categories that they BOTH belong to.

_____
_____

5.G.4

34. Dennis biked 8 km and Patrick ran 6,172 m. Who traveled farther and by how much?
_____
_____

5.MD.1

139

ASSESSMENT

Figure X is shown below. Each cube in Figure X is 1 m³. Use the drawing to answer questions 35 - 36.

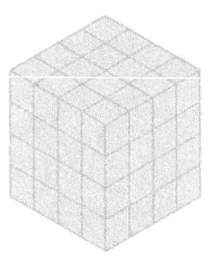

Figure X

= 1 m³

35. What is the volume of Figure X?

_____

_____

5.MD.4

36. Figure Y has $\frac{3}{4}$ as many cubes as Figure X. What is the volume of Figure Y?

_____

_____

5.MD.4

The table below shows the cost of some apples. Use the table to answer questions 37 – 38.

Apples	Cost (dollars)
2	4
4	8
6	12

37. What is the cost for 3 apples?

_____

_____

5.OA.3

38. What would you expect the cost of 9 apples to be?

_____

_____

5.OA.3

39. What is $30 - 21\frac{3}{5}$?

_____

_____

5.NF.1

ASSESSMENT

40. If Lane and his 3 brothers each ate $\frac{3}{4}$ of a potato, how many potatoes were there to start with?

_____

_____

5.NF.3

Use the rectangular prisms shown below to answer questions 41 – 43.
Figure A + Figure B = Figure C and each cube equals 1 cubic inch.

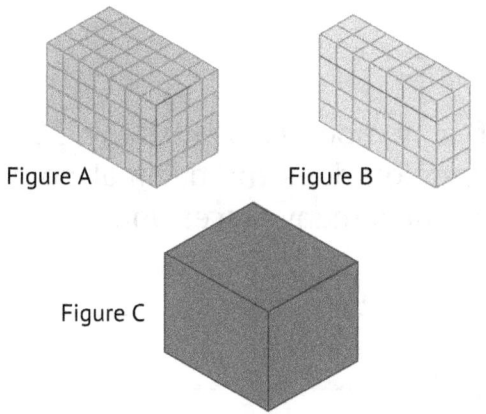

Figure A   Figure B

Figure C

41. What is the volume of Figure A?

_____

_____

5.MD.5

42. What is the volume of Figure B?

_____

_____

5.MD.5

43. What is the volume of Figure C?

_____

_____

5.MD.5

44. Xander thought that $\frac{4}{5} + \frac{7}{8}$ equaled $\frac{11}{13}$. How do you know this answer is incorrect?

_____

_____

5.NF.2

ASSESSMENT

45. The shaded part of the square below has a length of $\frac{5}{7}$ inch and a width of $\frac{1}{2}$ inch.

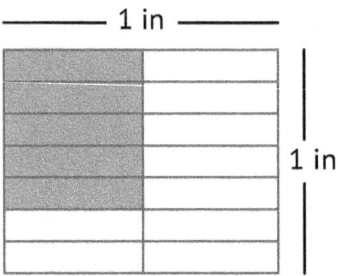

What is the area, in square inches, of the shaded part of the square?

_____

5.NF.4

46. What are all of the categories that BOTH shapes below belong to?

_____
_____

5.G.4

47. Twenty-six bowling balls weigh 302 pounds. The number of pounds per bowling ball is between what 2 numbers?

_____
_____

5.NF.3

48. If a number is divided by 10^4, which direction does the decimal point move and how many places does it move?

_____
_____

5.NBT.2

142

ANSWER KEY

VIDEO EXPLANATIONS

ANSWER KEY

WEEK 1

DAY 1	DAY 2	DAY 3	DAY 4	DAY 5
1. B	1. D	1. C	1. D	1. C
2. C	2. B	2. D	2. B	2. C
3. A	3. A	3. A	3. A	3. A
4. A	4. D	4. A	4. C	4. C
5. D	5. B	5. C	5. D	5. D
6. C		6. B	6. D	6. A

WEEK 2

DAY 1	DAY 2	DAY 3	DAY 4	DAY 5
1. A	1. C	1. A	1. C	1. B
2. D	2. B	2. D	2. A	2. A
3. C	3. D	3. A	3. D	3. D
4. B	4. C	4. B	4. B	4. A
5. A	5. A	5. C	5. C	5. C
6. D	6. C	6. D	6. B	

WEEK 3

DAY 1	DAY 2	DAY 3	DAY 4	DAY 5
1. C	1. B	1. B	1. D	1. C
2. C	2. D	2. D	2. B	2. B
3. A	3. A	3. C	3. D	3. A
4. D	4. B	4. B	4. C	4. D
5. C	5. C	5. C	5. B	5. C
6. B				6. C

WEEK 4

DAY 1	DAY 2	DAY 3	DAY 4	DAY 5
1. A	1. C	1. B	1. D	1. B
2. B	2. A	2. C	2. C	2. C
3. C	3. D	3. C	3. B	3. A
4. B	4. D	4. B	4. A	4. B
5. B	5. C	5. A	5. D	5. D
6. D	6. B	6. D	6. C	6. D

WEEK 5

DAY 1	DAY 2	DAY 3	DAY 4	DAY 5
1. D	1. B	1. A	1. A	1. B
2. A	2. C	2. C	2. D	2. A
3. C	3. D	3. D	3. B	3. B
4. B	4. C	4. D	4. D	4. C
5. D	5. C	5. B	5. C	5. D
6. C	6. B	6. B	6. C	6. A

WEEK 6

DAY 1	DAY 2	DAY 3	DAY 4	DAY 5
1. A	1. C	1. B	1. B	1. D
2. A	2. B	2. C	2. C	2. C
3. A	3. A	3. C	3. B	3. A
4. B	4. D	4. A	4. D	4. C
5. D	5. C	5. D	5. B	
6. D	6. B			

ANSWER KEY

WEEK 7

DAY 1	DAY 2	DAY 3	DAY 4	DAY 5
1. C	1. B	1. C	1. C	1. D
2. A	2. D	2. D	2. A	2. B
3. D	3. A	3. A	3. D	3. B
4. C	4. D	4. D	4. D	4. C
5. D	5. C	5. C	5. A	5. C
6. C	6. B	6. A	6. C	

WEEK 8

DAY 1	DAY 2	DAY 3	DAY 4	DAY 5
1. C	1. C	1. A	1. A	1. C
2. C	2. D	2. D	2. B	2. D
3. B	3. A	3. D	3. D	3. A
4. D	4. B	4. B	4. B	4. D
5. C		5. C	5. D	5. A

WEEK 9

DAY 1	DAY 2	DAY 3	DAY 4	DAY 5
1. B	1. D	1. A	1. B	1. A
2. B	2. C	2. C	2. A	2. C
3. C	3. B	3. C	3. A	3. A
4. B	4. A	4. D	4. B	4. B
5. B	5. A	5. C	5. C	5. B
6. A	6. B			6. D

WEEK 10

DAY 1	DAY 2	DAY 3	DAY 4	DAY 5
1. B	1. C	1. D	1. B	1. A
2. D	2. D	2. A	2. C	2. C
3. C	3. D	3. B	3. D	3. C
4. B	4. B	4. B	4. D	4. B
5. A	5. A	5. D	5. D	5. D
			6. A	

WEEK 11

DAY 1	DAY 2	DAY 3	DAY 4	DAY 5
1. D	1. D	1. C	1. C	1. A
2. C	2. B	2. A	2. A	2. A
3. B	3. A	3. A	3. C	3. A
4. B	4. B	4. B	4. B	4. B
5. A	5. B	5. D	5. C	5. D
6. C	6. B	6. C	6. D	

WEEK 12

DAY 1	DAY 2	DAY 3	DAY 4	DAY 5
1. B	1. B	1. D	1. A	1. C
2. C	2. A	2. A	2. A	2. C
3. A	3. D	3. D	3. D	3. A
4. D	4. C	4. C	4. D	4. C
5. B	5. D	5. A	5. B	5. B
			6. B	6. B

145

ANSWER KEY

WEEK 13

DAY 1	DAY 2	DAY 3	DAY 4	DAY 5
1. B	1. C	1. B	1. A	1. D
2. A	2. A	2. A	2. D	2. B
3. D	3. A	3. D	3. B	3. C
4. B	4. C	4. A	4. A	4. C
5. D	5. D	5. D	5. B	5. D
6. D	6. D		6. D	6. D

WEEK 14

DAY 1	DAY 2	DAY 3	DAY 4	DAY 5
1. D	1. B	1. C	1. B	1. C
2. B	2. A	2. C	2. C	2. A
3. A	3. D	3. A	3. C	3. A
4. C	4. A	4. A	4. A	4. C
5. C	5. C	5. C	5. A	5. D
		6. B		

WEEK 15

DAY 1	DAY 2	DAY 3	DAY 4	DAY 5
1. D	1. C	1. B	1. B	1. B
2. D	2. D	2. B	2. A	2. D
3. B	3. B	3. C	3. C	3. C
4. D	4. B	4. D	4. C	4. D
5. A	5. D	5. B		5. A
6. A	6. D			6. B

WEEK 16

DAY 1	DAY 2	DAY 3	DAY 4	DAY 5
1. C	1. C	1. C	1. D	1. D
2. D	2. D	2. C	2. B	2. B
3. C	3. D	3. D	3. C	3. C
4. D	4. C	4. D	4. D	4. A
5. B	5. B	5. A	5. A	5. D
			6. B	

WEEK 17

DAY 1	DAY 2	DAY 3	DAY 4	DAY 5
1. B	1. D	1. C	1. B	1. B
2. C	2. C	2. A	2. A	2. A
3. B	3. B	3. B	3. D	3. C
4. D	4. A	4. A	4. D	4. C
		5. D	5. C	5. B
		6. B		6. A

WEEK 18

DAY 1	DAY 2	DAY 3	DAY 4	DAY 5
1. D	1. A	1. B	1. C	1. D
2. C	2. C	2. A	2. D	2. D
3. A	3. B	3. D	3. B	3. C
4. C	4. D	4. D	4. B	4. D
5. B	5. D		5. C	5. C
6. C				6. A

ANSWER KEY

WEEK 19

DAY 1	DAY 2	DAY 3	DAY 4	DAY 5
1. B	1. A	1. A	1. B	1. C
2. C	2. D	2. B	2. A	2. A
3. D	3. C	3. B	3. C	3. B
4. C	4. B	4. C	4. D	4. B
5. D	5. D	5. D	5. B	5. C
6. A	6. A			

WEEK 20

DAY 1	DAY 2	DAY 3	DAY 4	DAY 5
1. D	1. B	1. D	1. B	1. D
2. C	2. C	2. A	2. D	2. C
3. B	3. D	3. B	3. A	3. D
4. D	4. A	4. B	4. D	4. D
5. C	5. C	5. A	5. C	5. C
6. A	6. C	6. C		

Challenge Questions

WEEK 1

A. a) 1,496,800 and b) 149,680,000
B. a) 149.68 and b) 1.4968

WEEK 2

$(2 \times 100) + (4 \times 10) + (5 \times 1) + \left(1 \times \frac{1}{100}\right) + \left(6 \times \frac{1}{1000}\right)$

WEEK 3

108,830

WEEK 4

87.152 + 37.918 = 125.07 or 37.918 + 87.152 = 125.07

WEEK 5

(5 × 7) − 12 NOT 12 − (5 × 7)

WEEK 6

2 + (12 × 3) or (12 × 3) + 2

WEEK 7

$8\frac{7}{24}$

WEEK 8

$\frac{1}{4} < \frac{1}{2}$ and $\frac{1}{4} < \frac{1}{3}$ so when $\frac{1}{2}$ and $\frac{1}{3}$ are added together, they should equal more than $\frac{1}{4}$.

ANSWER KEY

WEEK 9
9 miles

WEEK 10
$\frac{5}{24}$ yds^2

WEEK 11
The product would be greater than $\frac{7}{8}$ but less than 7.

WEEK 12
Nichole spent 7 hours and Nate spent $1\frac{1}{6}$ hours.

WEEK 13
$\frac{7}{40}$ of a box

WEEK 14
$42.33

WEEK 15
7,100 m or 7.1 km

25 × 5 × 2 or 5 × 5 × 10

WEEK 16
If the 3 numbers given by the student equal 250 when multiplied, the answer is correct. Some examples:

WEEK 17
9 cubic meters

WEEK 18
4,464 cm^3

WEEK 19
B = (3, 10) or (3, 0)

WEEK 20
Both shapes have 4 equal sides, 2 pairs of parallel lines, opposite sides are equal, opposite angles are equal and they are both quadrilaterals.

ANSWER KEY

Assessment

1. A
2. B
3. A
4. B
5. D
6. C
7. B
8. A
9. D
10. A
11. C
12. D
13. C
14. B
15. B
16. C
17. A
18. C
19. D
20. C
21. D
22. C
23. B
24. D
25. B
26. A
27. D
28. D
29. C
30. (5, 3)
31. Bear and Cougar
32. Aardvark
33. They are both quadrilaterals and parallelograms.
34. Dennis traveled 1,828 m farther.
35. 64 m³
36. 48 m³
37. $6
38. $18
39. $8\frac{2}{5}$
40. 3
41. 112 in³
42. 56 in³
43. 168 in³
44. Answers may vary and can include:

    a. $\frac{7}{8} > \frac{11}{13}$ so the answer should be something more than $\frac{11}{13}$.

    b. The LCD of 5 and 8 is 40, not 13.

    c. $\frac{4}{5}$ and $\frac{7}{8}$ are close to 1 so when adding them the answer should be > 1.

45. $\frac{5}{14}$ in²
46. They both are quadrilaterals and have at least 1 pair of parallel lines.
47. 11 and 12
48. The decimal point moves 4 places to the left.

KIDS WINTER ACADEMY

Kids Winter Academy by ArgoPrep covers material learned in September through December so your child can reinforce the concepts they should have learned in class. We recommend using this particular series during the winter break. These workbooks include two weeks of activities for math, reading, science, and social studies. Best of all, you can access detailed video explanations to all the questions on our website.

SOCIAL STUDIES

Social Studies Daily Practice Workbook by ArgoPrep allows students to build foundational skills and review concepts. Our workbooks explore social studies topics in depth with ArgoPrep's 5 E's to build social studies mastery.

Want free K-8 **math** and **English** worksheets?
Visit us at:
argoprep.com/worksheets

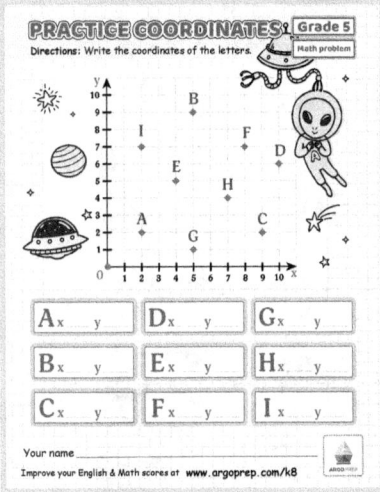

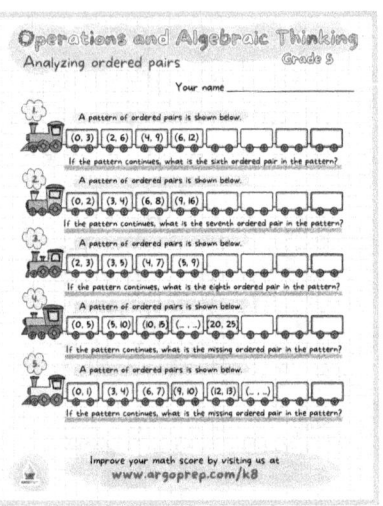

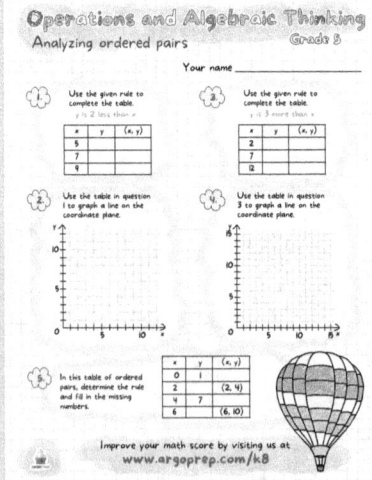
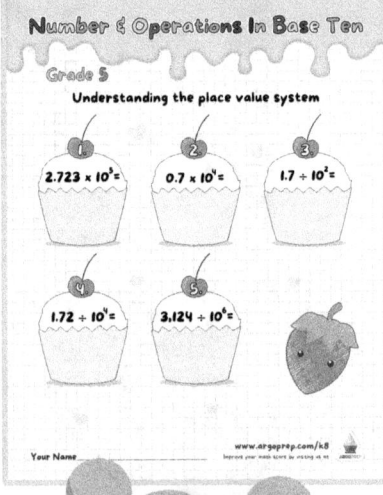

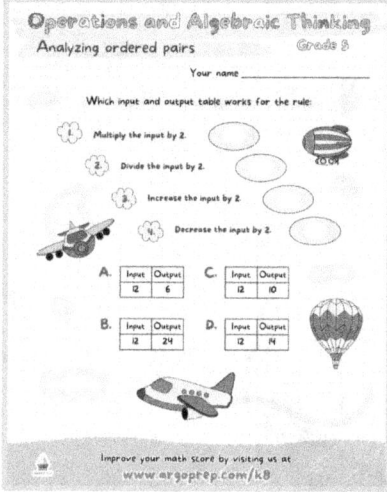
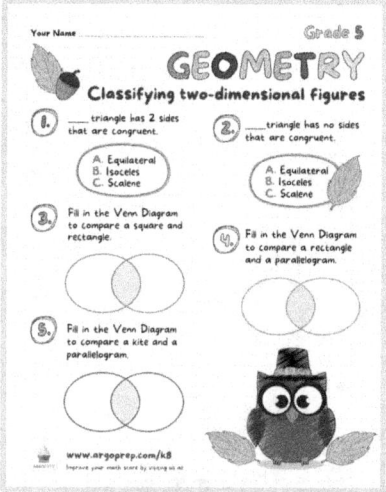
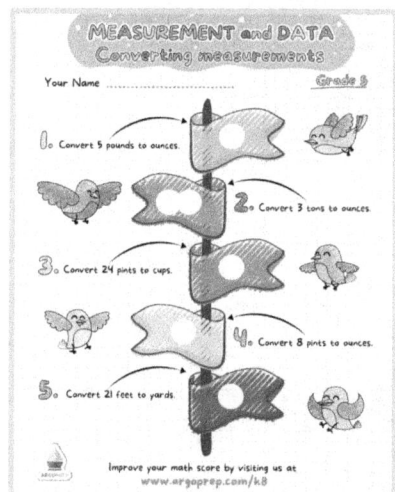
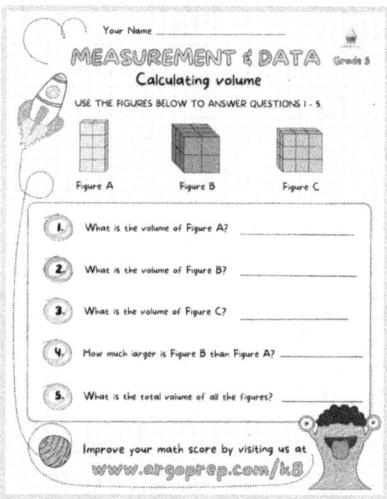

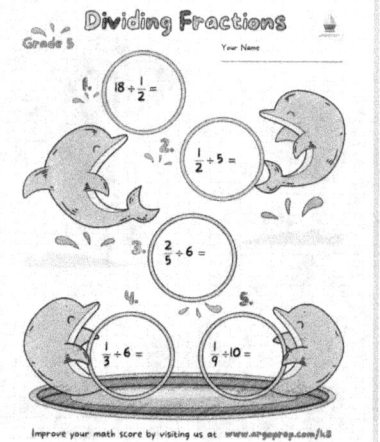
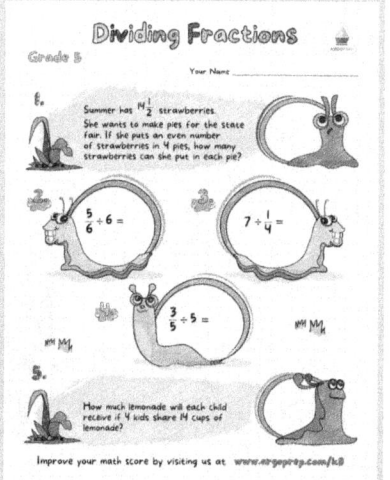

DIPLOMA

The certificate is presented to:

_____
your name

_____
by school name

for successful completion of ArgoPrep's Grade 5 workbook

_____
Signature

_____
Date

5th Grade

Excellent work!

argoprep.com

www.ingramcontent.com/pod-product-compliance
Lightning Source LLC
Chambersburg PA
CBHW051804100526
44592CB00016B/2554